BETKA ZAMOYSKA

THE TEN POUND FARE

EXPERIENCES OF BRITISH PEOPLE
WHO EMIGRATED
TO AUSTRALIA IN THE 1950S

VIKING

For Michael and Anna

VIKING

Published by the Penguin Group
27 Wrights Lane, London w8 5tz, England
Viking Penguin Inc., 40 West 23rd Street, New York, New York 10010, USA
Penguin Books Australia Ltd, Ringwood, Victoria, Australia
Penguin Books Canada Ltd, 2801 John Street, Markham, Ontario, Canada l3r 1b4
Penguin Books (NZ) Ltd, 182–190 Wairau Road, Auckland 10, New Zealand

Penguin Books Ltd, Registered Offices: Harmondsworth, Middlesex, England

First published 1988

Copyright © Betka Zamoyska, 1988

Printed in Great Britain by
Richard Clay Ltd, Bungay, Suffolk
Filmset in Garamond

A CIP catalogue record for this book is available from the Britsh Library

ISBN 0-670-81963-8

CONTENTS

ARAFURA

TIMOR
SEA

MELVILLE I.
BATHURST I.

BÊCHE DE MER

DARWIN

Cotton

Daly R.

PEARL

WYNDHAM

Victoria R.

Gold

VICTORIA
DOWNS

NEWCA
WATER

Cattle

DERBY

Sandalwood

NORTH

Sheep   Fitzroy R.

BROOME

Cattle Raising Area

TERRI

P. HEDLAND

Gold

Tin   Copper

de Grey R.

SHELL

WESTERN

ONSLOW

ROEBOURNE

Fortescue R.

SO

INDIAN

Ashburton R.

AUSTRALIA

Gold

Sheep

AUSTR

OOLDEA

CARNARVON

Gascoyne

Sheep

WILUNA

Gold

SHELL

SOLE

OCEAN

Murchison R.

Cattle

Sheep Raising Area

Wheat

GERALDTON

Gold

Sheep

EUCLA

SNAPPER

Copper   KALGOORLIE

COOLGARDIE   Silver

Sheep
Wheat   Zinc

PERTH   Lead

FREMANTLE   Fruit

Hay & Oats

Timber
Jarrah

ESPERANCE

Coal   Sheep
Karri

ALBANY

SOUTHERN OCEA

AUSTRALIA

ACKNOWLEDGE-MENTS

Grateful thanks for their help to:
R. T. Appleyard, the Australian High Commission, Don Boyd, Michael and Anna Browne, Norman Hoffman, the London Library, Nicky Ryde, Frances Wilks, and particularly to the Ten Pound Poms whose memories are recorded here.

I would also like to thank all those who contributed to the illustrations, specially Lorna Groom, J. R. Holt, John Titterton, David Wheatley, and Susan Rose-Smith for her excellent picture research.

The publisher would like to credit the cartoons on p. xvi (*The Bulletin*, 19 February 1947), p. 65 (*The Age*, 18 July 1967), p. 156 George Molnar, *Insubstantial Pageant*, Angus & Robertson, 1959).

LIST OF PLATES

FOREWORD

It is perhaps worth looking back a little at the historic context of the Assisted Passage Scheme, placing it in the light of what preceded it, before trying to sum up the experience.

After Captain Cook's *Voyages*, one of the most vivid early eye-witness accounts of British settlers in Australia was Charles Darwin's. He visited Australia nearly fifty years after the first fleet and wrote about his impressions in *The Voyage of the Beagle* (1839). He favourably contrasted the results of fifty years of colonization in Australia with several centuries of South American colonization, greatly to the advantage of the former. He noticed the growing tension between the convicts – and their descendants – and the free settlers, regarded as interlopers by the convicts. The settlers had been coming out to New South Wales from quite early days in the colony's history, usually to take up grants of land from the Government. Some were West Country farmers and others were young, retired officers and their wives, particularly from India. Darwin foresaw that Australia would progress beyond being a raw material producer to become a dominant trading force in the Pacific. He concluded that New South Wales was 'a colony of which Rome might have been proud'.

What Darwin did not foresee was the Ballarat gold rush and the rise of Melbourne, about fifteen years later. This was accompanied by a mass immigration of gold seekers who numerically tipped the scales decisively in favour of the free settlers.

During the gold rush years, the Australian population almost doubled in this short time, although the problem of returnees soon emerged. There were many disillusioned returnees who went back to Britain poorer than they had been when they set off. Two articulate and unlikely ones were Thomas Woolner, the pre-Raphaelite sculptor, who discovered no gold but made some money doing portrait heads of those more fortunate than himself, and Henry Kingsley, the novelist, who found enough gold to get himself home again after three years in Australia, where he also gathered material for two of his best books *Geoffrey Hamlyn* and *The Hillyars and the Burtons*. The discovery of gold was perhaps the outstanding event of the second fifty years of Australian colonization.

The third fifty years covered Australia's involvement in the South African War and then in the 1914–18 War, in which the Australians played a full part, fighting as part of the British forces in the Dardanelles and in France. By the end of this period, before the Second World War, the five original separate colonies of New South Wales, Victoria, South Australia, Queensland and Western Australia had federated. The Commonwealth Government – the Government of Australia – had acquired full Dominion status which, with very limited exceptions, did away with the power of the British parliament to legislate for any of the Dominions. About the same time, the British Government and the Commonwealth Government went off the gold standard and, instead of both currencies being based on the gold sovereign of identical weight and fineness (whether minted in Australia or England), they developed their own paper currencies which ceased to be of identical value. During this period, too, the agreement of the Dominion Governments had to be obtained for any change in the succession to the English throne. This prolonged and complicated the negotiations about the abdication of Edward VIII as the British Government could not pass the Abdication Act without the consent of the Dominions.

The fourth fifty-year period, just ended, started as an even more troubled time. It began with the 1939–45 War. The Australian Commonwealth declared war with Germany on its own account at virtually the same time as the British Government, and again Australia played a very full part, both in Greece and North Africa and, after the entry of Japan into the war at the end of 1941, very much nearer home. At the peak of the Japanese offensive they bombed Darwin and almost reached Port Moresby at the south-eastern tip of New Guinea. And, with the fall of Singapore, it became painfully apparent that Australia could no longer rely on the British Navy for its defence against external aggression. The major role in the Pacific war was, in fact, borne by the Americans, although the Australian army fought its way back to the north coast of New Guinea well before the end of the war.

Looking ahead to the Korean War and to Vietnam, it is worth recording that although both Australia and Great Britain sent a substantial contingent to Korea, only the Australians took part in the Vietnam War.

Against this general background, the Assisted Passage Scheme looks very much like a last great imperial gesture, conceived in terms of imperial grand strategy along with the British Maralinga rocket range in the central Australian desert and the early atomic weapon tests there.

It is also worth noting that both the British Prime Minister Clement Attlee and the Australian Minister John Curtin had been in the Cabinet almost throughout the Second World War, and that they and their advisers would have thought naturally in terms of imperial strategy. But, whatever its origins, the Scheme turned into something very different from this imperial objective. It led to a great growth in the Australian economy, to other European immigration and to an increased sense of Australian national identity.

The documented extracts in this book show what the experience meant to some of those who took part in the Assisted Passage Scheme, telling how many settled happily in their new country, finding they had secured a better life for themselves and their children in a better climate and a better environment, but how a few faced similar problems to those experienced by the returnees from the gold rush. Yet the overwhelming impression one gets is that the Scheme was a success, both in the numbers who came and stayed in Australia and in their feelings about doing so.

The decision to emigrate depended on a multiplicity of choices and personal, sometimes almost accidental, decisions, but the Scheme itself was the agent which made these choices and decisions possible. Curiously, the rather depressed state of the United Kingdom, with rationing and power failures continuing for some years after the end of the War, does not seem to have influenced the decision to emigrate as much as might have been expected. People usually decided to emigrate more for personal than for practical reasons.

It is interesting to remember that another wave of immigrants was arriving over the same period as the British. These 'New Australians', Greeks, Italians, Ukrainians and others – many of them displaced in the course of Hitler's war – added new cultural strands to Australian life. Even the most hard-shelled old Australians seemed to accept their contributions to the greatly improved range of restaurants and delicatessens, as well as acknowledging their significant part in the wave of building construction and projects such as the Snowy River scheme.

In the arts and literature, as well as in business, Australia has taken off, possibly because of this rapid growth of population. With a novelist of the stature of Patrick White and an artist of the calibre of Sidney Nolan Australians can look anyone in the face. They have also had world-class singers since the days of the gold rush and the opening of the Melbourne Opera House. But the Sydney Opera House became a particular symbol of this cultural confidence. And, in the art world, as is so often the case, the major figures are the visible parts of a movement including many lesser, but by no means negligible, figures and Sydney became full of little art galleries. So, too, did the decorative arts flourish: the Alamein fountain and the Australian Navy's Chapel on the Cliffs are two impressive memorials to the 1939–45 War which equal United Kingdom memorials such as the Stanley Spencer chapel at Burghclere, commissioned after the First World War.

My own contacts with Australia and the Pacific region generally go back to the closing years of the

'And ye shall dispossess the inhabitants of the land, and dwell therein: for I have given you the land to possess it'

1939–45 War when I was serving in a section of the War Office concerned with this area. I have also had personal links with younger relatives who have emigrated to Australia from England over the last thirty years or have gone to work there. Several have now married and their children are very much Australian. While visiting Australia, I was struck by the kindness I received from the people, both new settlers and old, and felt, in spite of the growth of independence and the difference in life-style which this has brought about, that links with the United Kingdom remain strong. The Australians cherish their history and, as the ties between Britain and Australia have existed over such a long period, I feel that, however far it progressed from its original purposes, the Assisted Passage Scheme will have strengthened the links between the two countries.

I am fascinated by the details of how the Scheme worked, and of the contrasts between Australia now and then, which emerge from the personal accounts of the Ten Pound Poms. Unlike modern travellers to Australia who jet over there in a matter of hours, most of the Ten Pound migrants of the Fifties set off on a long sea voyage to what was then a very distant land.

MICHAEL BROWNE

INTRODUCTION

The decision to emigrate is an intensely personal one. After twenty-eight years as an Australian migration officer, including fifteen years spent overseas, I have formed the view that there are as many reasons for emigration as there are emigrants.

Each person has an individualized balance sheet of 'push' and 'pull' factors on which their decision to leave the home country and forge a new life elsewhere is based. Some of these are, of course, common to all. In Australia's case, 'pull' factors include climate, life-style, presence of relatives or friends, work opportunities and a better future for children. 'Push' factors may include the weather, limited work prospects, inadequacies of health care and the adverse impact of close relatives. Of course, all these elements are based on perceptions which all too frequently can be inaccurate and unrealistic. For that reason, those who succeed in a new country (or at least suffer from a minimum of disruption to their everyday lives) are usually those whose expectations were well based in the first place.

Migration is not for the faint-hearted. It requires courage, foresight, patience, flexibility and, above all, determination. Those who emigrate merely to escape from problems in their homeland invariably find that they have taken these with them and, with the additional impact of the migration experience itself, they are more prone to failure. No statistics are kept on the number of migrants who have left Australia but recent estimates put it as high as 15 per cent. Certainly, many having returned to Britain want to go back to Australia but the problem of finding the funds and, most importantly, meeting the migration requirements a second time are very hard to overcome.

The million or more British migrants who accepted Australia's offer to migrate for only £10 over thirty years or so included a high proportion who had had very limited life-styles in Britain. Most had not travelled far beyond their front doors and few had been abroad. As a result, their perceptions of Australia, and of living in a foreign land, were frequently based on what they had read in the official leaflets or in newspapers and what their friends and relatives told them of their own experiences.

Unfortunately, while the official leaflets on such subjects as housing, health, education and social services were carefully worded to provide as accurate a picture as possible, in reality most prospective migrants believed what they wanted to, ignoring or downplaying the information which did not fit the picture they had created.

The views and reports of friends and relatives presented another difficulty and sometimes had devastating effects. All too often they rationalized their own experiences in a way which ignored early problems and added gloss to their own success story. Others were trying simply to persuade those back home to join them, raising expectations to fanciful levels and making

Booklet No. 27

Australia Offers

ASSISTED PASSAGES UNDER THE
COMMONWEALTH NOMINATION SCHEME

*Government pamphlets formed part of the Scheme's migrant information
policy*

the reality of the migration experience even more oner-
ous to cope with.

Migration is not easy for anyone but it is far more
difficult for the old than for the young. Ageing parents
often accompany their families to Australia or join them
later not because they want to emigrate but because
they want to be near them. The intrinsic problems of
aged migrants in Australia have been studied in depth
and are well documented. Invariably they include the
generation gap with children and, more particularly,
grandchildren, which tends to widen as the young
quickly adopt new social customs and cast aside those
social mores on which life in their homeland was based.
If the children were born in Australia, the differences
can be even more pronounced.

Of course the children mostly adapt very quickly to
an Australian life-style with its emphasis on outdoor
living and a freer way of life. The younger they are, the
better, as the transition from one education system to
another is often not a simple one for the older teenager
also trying to cope with the pressures of growing up.

My overwhelming impression of the Ten Pound migrants I met is of people with few funds or possessions
often leaving council houses and a highly protective
environment with health care and social security built
in. The relative few who owned houses had often lived
in them for years and many had simply continued to
live in the old family home.

Australian migration officers were located at many
points around Britain to make the job of visiting an
Australian office as easy and as inexpensive as possible.
In addition, a large team of selection officers interviewed people at labour offices. They underwent health
and character checks and, provided that these were

clear, they could be on their way to Australia in a few months. Early travellers went in ships leased by the Australian Government to carry migrants from Britain and Europe, while later ones went by air. Some say the transition to Australia was eased by the long sea voyage and that the flight was far too taxing for those unused to such travel and translated migrants far too quickly from one environment to another. On arrival most went to migrant centres with heavily subsidized accommodation and food. For many these were ugly, uncomfortable places which they could not wait to escape from; it was almost impossible to persuade others to leave, as they clung to the security the situation offered.

The settling-in experience was almost always worse for wives. Husbands were generally quickly placed in employment and had the accompanying opportunities to make new friends and get to know the country. On the other hand, wives had to cope with the continuing pressures around them and, as one might expect, many suffered from homesickness, which quickly spread in the migrant centre environment. For a few it became so horrendous that it led to mental breakdown and eventual repatriation of them and their families to the UK at Australian Government expense. They were prohibited from returning to Australia for at least five years and, in reality, most never managed to return although some dearly wanted to. Their perceptions of life at home were often as deficient as those original ones of life in Australia and were quickly dispelled.

For some, however, the uncertainty prevailed. A near neighbour of mine in Canberra had moved backwards and forwards to Australia seven times largely because of his wife's inability to settle in either country.

Typically, all of the substantial travel funds needed to move the family and their belongings across the world came from money earned in Australia. He freely admitted that he could never save money while in Britain.

One of the rules which applied to the Ten Pound migrants was that they had to remain in Australia for at least two years or they were required to repay all or part of the Australian Government's contribution to their fare. Those migrants who did return home frequently became Australian supporters who persuaded others to consider emigration.

The Assisted Passage represented to many people an exciting and inexpensive working-holiday for two years. Our experience was, however, that many people who said they were going for the adventure actually stayed and became first-class migrants. One obvious reason for their success was the relative lack of pressure on them to succeed at all costs in those early years.

The Ten Pound Scheme worked admirably in achieving its twin objectives of providing Australia with much-needed people, while at the same time offering better opportunities to Britons. Of course there were problems, a few of which I have alluded to here. But as Betka Zamoyska's revealing, in-depth interviews with some of the people themselves so vividly show, this migration programme mostly produced the results which the Australian Government advertisements and posters claimed – a better climate, better prospects for families and improved opportunities.

Those who succeeded sometimes did so in quite dramatic fashion. Migrants with nothing to lose and the will to make good quickly could achieve remarkable success almost overnight. Australian-born workers clinging to the security of jobs and a settled social environment were forced to recognize that the migrants brought with them some positive attitudes which were missing among Australians. Some, naturally, were less well received and the so-called 'whingeing Poms' were frowned upon by Australians and other ethnic groups

They'll help make Australia great.

alike. Those who 'whinged' were often young married couples who had grown used to the welfare state in the U K and found the relative lack of government support in Australia very difficult to come to terms with. Also frowned upon were some of the British-born shop stewards in factories (particularly in the motor vehicle industry) who found they could exercise a powerful influence over the attitudes of workers and, at the same time, develop a power base which they had not had in their homeland.

The British migrants of today, mostly young, educated, professionally or technically qualified people with substantial funds, bear little relation to the Ten Pound migrants. They find it fairly easy to buy a house and obtain work. They also return for visits to Britain at fairly regular intervals. In other words, many of the pressures faced by their less well-educated and less pre-pared counterparts of fifteen to forty years ago do not exist for them.

Australians and British have been enriched by the experience. Readers of Betka Zamoyska's highly informa-tive and entertaining study of the Ten Pound migrants will also be enriched. Migration builds countries and shapes people. It is one of the most remarkable areas of human endeavour and will always have an enormous impact on people and places.

NORMAN HOFFMAN
Regional Director (Migration)
Britain and Ireland
Australian High Commission
London

1

A TICKET TO A NEW LIFE

After almost six years of war – black-outs, sleepless nights in bomb-shelters and long, cold queues waiting for a small ration of meat or coal – many civilians in Britain must have wondered whether peace was any better. Rationing continued well into the mid-Fifties (and petrol rationing was re-introduced after the Suez crisis); there were no more bombs but many of the bombed-out homes stood desolate for years; unfilled craters left constant reminders of the War and some particularly bleak winters in the late 1940s must have added to the general sense of desolation. Ex-servicemen returned from the Front to face the prospect of unemployment and for many there was a desperate hunt for a home. Housing was scarce and many of the houses still standing were in poor condition. The strict exchange controls meant that few could escape from the drabness of post-war Britain for a holiday in the sun. Cheap package holidays had not yet come into existence. For all its horrors, the War had given many a sense of adventure, a taste for travel and the experience of living from day to day and learning to cope with changing circumstances. The return to a daily routine with few luxuries to enhance the monotony of life must have been a gloomy prospect. It is not surprising that when the first advertisements appeared offering people a new life and better work prospects in sunny Australia there was an enormous rush of interest.

If British people felt the need for Australia, Australia felt a still greater need for the British. Although Australians have always been conscious of their small population in relation to their vast land mass, it was not until after the threat of invasion from the Japanese during the Second World War that they realized there was an urgent need for them to increase their numbers at a rapid rate. Arthur Calwell, Minister for Immigration, made a statement in the House of Representatives in August 1945 which showed the Australian Government's concern about its dwindling population:

> If Australians have learned one lesson from the Pacific War now moving to a successful conclusion, it is surely that we cannot continue to hold our island continent for ourselves and our descendants unless we greatly increase our numbers. We are but 7,000,000 people and we hold 3,000,000 square miles of this earth's surface. Our coastline extends for 12,000 miles and our density of population is only 2.5 persons per square mile. Much of our land is situated within a rain belt of less than 10 inches per annum and this area is, therefore, largely uninhabitable. In those parts more favourably situated, much development and settlement have yet to be undertaken. Our need to undertake it is urgent and imperative if we are to survive. While the world yearns for peace and abhors war, no one can guarantee that there will be no more war. A third world war is not impossible, and after a period of fitful peace, humanity may be face to face again with the horrors of another period of total war.

Although immigration seemed the obvious answer,

Calwell pointed out that the Government's immigration policy would be carefully planned and
the influx of immigrants would be restricted to a
number that the Australian economy could absorb at
any time:

> People who talk glibly about bringing millions of
> people to Australia in relatively short periods have
> no conception of either the physical or the economic
> factors that operate in an expanding population. It has
> been proven by hard experience over long periods
> that the maximum effective population absorption
> capacity in any expanding country is usually some-
> where about two per cent of its numbers. This figure
> includes the net increase of population, either by
> the excess of births over deaths, or the excess of
> arrivals over departures, or a combination of both.
> Two per cent of the present Australian population is
> approximately 140,000. The net increase, being the ex-
> cess of births over deaths, has averaged during the last
> five years, approximately 70,000 a year. This would
> leave, therefore, a migration ceiling of 70,000 a
> year, assuming that the economy was fully expanded
> to take the maximum number. It is obvious, there-
> fore, that any suggestion to treble or even double the
> population within a generation is not likely to be
> realized. In view of the alarming fall in the birth-
> rate, and the decline of the average Australian family
> from six children in 1875 to three children in 1925,
> and then to slightly over two children at present,
> our immediate problem will be to hold our popula-
> tion figures without some migration.

Later, the defence argument tended to be overlooked

in favour of the more practical economic reasons for immigration, but it acted as a spur for Australia to set up an immigration policy.

The British and Australian Governments gradually worked out a policy for the Assisted Passage Scheme. They agreed to share the cost of transporting British migrants and a big appeal was launched to interest people in Australia. There were advertisements in the newspapers and posters to announce the forthcoming scheme. Before it began in earnest on 31 March 1947, there was a flood of letters to Australia House in London from people all over the country who were interested in emigrating. The 'Report of the Commonwealth Immigration Advisory Committee' stated that:

> From a perusal of applications and personal investigation and interview, the Committee is satisfied that first-class migrants are available in considerable numbers. The question of personnel and capacity of intending migrants has been dealt with in many reports from Australia House and the Committee found applications most numerous from
> a) Service units and discharged servicemen who fought alongside Australian servicemen, with many applications from N.C.O.s and junior officers with families well represented in the list, and from women in the services.
> b) People with relatives already in Australia who had done well and were anxious to bring out other members of their families.
> c) Civilians, war workers, technicians in all branches of industry, including those sections of industry which had a sudden expansion of effort as ancillary to the war effort.

One information officer who worked at Australia House when the first letters started to pour in said:

It was my duty to sort out the letters into different categories. The two main groups, which we were interested in sending out first of all, were ex-servicemen and their wives and children, and families who had relatives in Australia. Later on we sent out single people as well, but in the initial stages we were most interested in the response from those first two groups. We also got a lot of general queries about Australia. People wrote in asking about the climate, whether there were a lot of dangerous animals and insects, all kinds of things. When the scheme got going in earnest we then sent off application forms to all those who wrote in and, if they looked as if they were suitable, they were asked to come for an interview.

A team of information officers would go round the country and set up interview centres at the employment exchanges and arrange to see all the interviewees in one particular area. They only spent a few days in each place so the interviews were usually not longer than half an hour but this varied depending on the number of people interviewed. A medical officer went along with the team so he could conduct a medical examination at the same time. If the applicants were approved and were passed as medically fit they were then sent a letter saying that their application had been successful. They were asked to send in their ten pounds, except for the ex-servicemen and their families who travelled free. They were then told that they would be informed when a berth on a ship was available for them. An information officer explained:

The sort of qualities we were looking for in the first groups of migrants were whether they had the kind of skills and trades that would be required in Australia; whether they were adaptable and could cope with a different way of life and whether they would be the sort of people who would mix well with the Australians.

When the Scheme was first set up it came into operation for an initial period of two years. An Agreement was signed on 5 March 1946 between the Secretary of State for Dominion Affairs and the Government of Australia to carry out a scheme for joint assistance to British people going out to settle in Australia. Owing to a number of problems in setting up the Scheme, particularly the shortage of shipping, the first group of migrants did not set off until the end of March 1947. Arthur Calwell reported in 1949 that, when the Scheme first started:

> ... only four ships were available to carry migrants among tourist class passengers. There were no ships available for the exclusive carriage of migrants.
>
> In the first three months of the Scheme, the only sailings to Australia of ships carrying migrants were the *Largs Bay*, the *Wairingi*, the *Orion* and the *Strath-even*. Between them they carried 533 migrants — a rate of 2,212 new citizens for Australia a year.

Two years later, the position had improved and more ships were available. Calwell reported that:

> Today there are in sight 23 vessels of a total ton-

nage of 419,716 tons to help bring British migrants. Eleven, of a total tonnage of 201,320 tons, are already in service. By the end of this year we expect to have 21 ships totalling 366,292 tons in service.

Of these ships, eight will be exclusively for the carriage of migrants. In the other vessels, a far greater proportion of migrants' berths will be available than was available in sailings twelve months ago . . .

He then recounted the names and tonnage of the exclusively migrant ships, which ranged from the 27,269 ton *Georgic* to the 10,552 ton *Cheshire*, and the other ships on which a proportion of berths was allocated to migrants, including the *Orcades* of 31,000 tons and *Port Hobart* of 11,377. Another vessel, the 16,297 ton *Cameronia*, was being rebuilt at a cost of £500,000 to the Commonwealth Government of Australia but there was still not nearly enough shipping to meet the demand. So many ships had been damaged during the War that shipping of a suitable quality to transport British passengers was in short supply and it took time and money to refurbish the wartime aircraft-carriers that later made up the bulk of the migrant ships.

To encourage families to take advantage of the Scheme, special concessions were made for children. According to the 'Report of the Commonwealth Immigration Advisory Committee':

Each migrant of 19 years of age and over is required to contribute £10 towards the cost of a passage under the Scheme. For a juvenile of 14 but not more than 18 years of age the contribution is £5, and children under 14 years of age travel free. The

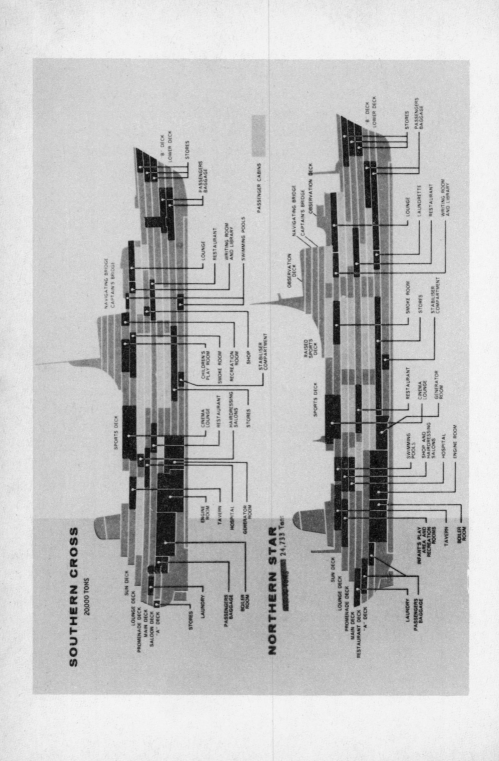

SOUTHERN CROSS
20,000 TONS

NORTHERN STAR   24,733 Tons

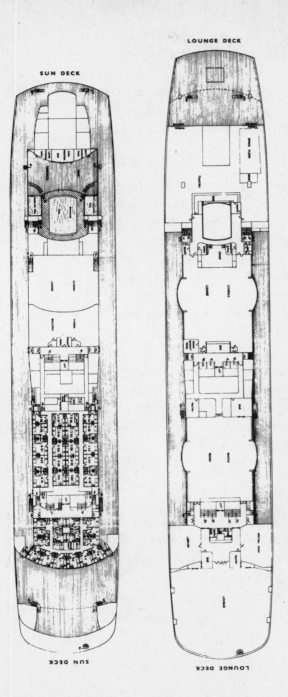
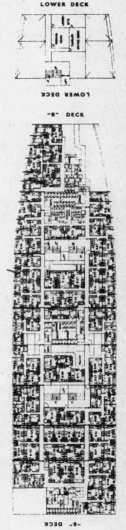

Three deck plans of the eight-deck ship, showing cramped migrant sleeping quarters on the lower deck

selection of assisted migrants is carried out by the
Australian immigration authorities in Britain, using
facilities for recruitment provided throughout the
country by the United Kingdom Government.
Should an assisted migrant wish to leave Australia
within two years of his arrival, he is liable to repay
the amount of assistance which he received for his
outward passage.

Later, still greater concessions were granted to children, allowing all those of nineteen years and under to
travel free with their parents. The Report also pointed
out that although the British Government first agreed
to finance the Scheme on a fifty-fifty basis with the
Australian Government, it later had to withdraw much
of its financial support. This did not affect the migrant's
contribution because the difference was made up by
the Australian Government.

At the outset it was agreed that the balance of the
cost of assisted passages under the Scheme should be
shared equally between the two Governments. It was
then expected that the average cost of a passage to
Australia would be about £70–75, which would cost
each Government, after deduction of the migrant's
contribution of £10, some £30–£32 10s. Before the
Agreement had been long in operation, however,
it became apparent that the actual cost of passages
(particularly on the migrant ships, which tended to
produce little revenue on the return voyage) would
be substantially above these figures. It was therefore
agreed between the two Governments that the
United Kingdom contribution towards each passage
should be limited to a maximum of 50 per cent,

calculated on a 'normal' fare of £75, i.e. £32 10s, the migrant's contribution would remain at £10, and the Australian Government would pay the excess.

Later the UK contribution was cut down still more:

From April 1950, it was arranged that the United Kingdom contribution towards an adult's fare would not exceed £25. In the following year it was decided that the Agreement should be renewed for a further period of three years, from 31 March, 1951, subject to a maximum contribution of £500,000 from the United Kingdom funds in each year. Owing to the further deterioration of the financial position of this country, it was necessary, early in 1952, to re-open the matter of the obligations of the United Kingdom Government under the Agreement and the Australian Government finally accepted an offer of a United Kingdom contribution of £150,000 a year for each of the remaining two years of the Agreement, i.e. up to the 31 March, 1954. This arrangement has now been extended as a temporary measure, until 31 March, 1955.

Although the British Government ended up by contributing only a nominal sum towards the Scheme the Report argues that the United Kingdom's real investment lay in the people themselves:

The invisible contribution which the United Kingdom makes in this transaction lies, of course, in the value of the human beings who leave this country and go to Australia to create wealth there. If they are just at the beginning of their productive life, the whole cost of their raising and training will have been borne here, and this country receives nothing directly in return for the considerable investment which every individual represents.

It may seem strange that the British Government was prepared to lose such a valuable human investment, especially since after the War young skilled men were in demand to help build up Britain's shattered industries, until the economic conditions improved, there was quite a high level of unemployment. The Government wanted to provide either training or employment for its ex-servicemen to repay them for their war service. The Assisted Passage Scheme fitted in well with these provisions although one of the most important factors was the role Britain saw herself playing in the Commonwealth.

The Report makes this quite clear:

Arguing purely from motives of self-interest, the Assisted Passage Scheme enables this country to influence and control one of the most important and significant streams of emigration to other parts of the Commonwealth, and also to obtain accurate information about the ages and occupations of the migrants which the United Kingdom is losing.

In our convinced opinion, however, the Assisted Passage Scheme cannot be judged wholly in terms of narrow national profit and loss. The Commonwealth functions as a political entity because, in many fields such as this, there is close, informal, but highly effective co-operation between its members. The Australian Government, as we heard from Mr Holt, places a high value on the Scheme, and for this reason alone we believe that the United Kingdom should continue to support it. We regret that financial difficulties make it necessary for the United Kingdom contribution to be reduced from £500,000 to £150,000 in 1952, and we consider that, at a time when our economic position appears to be stable and when Australia has again raised their immigration target to 100,000 migrants a year, it would be politically most undesirable to reduce the United Kingdom stake in this important operation. There are many countries which are anxious to send their surplus population to Australia, and machinery exists in the Intergovernmental Committee for European Migration which makes it possible for them to do so. Half Australia's immigrants now are drawn from the continent of Europe. If the United Kingdom is to continue to contribute to Australia's growth and to maintain the British connection, then a scheme subsidizing British migration must continue to exist alongside the machinery subsidizing with dollars emigration from the rest of Europe. This is the view of all the Australians who gave evidence to us and it is a view which we share as a Board . . .

. . . We recommend that the Scheme and the Assisted Passage Agreement be renewed in March, 1955, with, as an interim measure, a United Kingdom contribution of not less than £150,000.

Britain continued to support the Assisted Passage Scheme, which provided passages for British migrants until the early 1970s, but Calwell's original migration policy that 'for every foreign migrant there will be ten people from the United Kingdom' became less and less the case. By the middle of the 1950s it became evident that British immigration would never reach the levels

THE TEN POUND FARE

that Calwell had originally anticipated. In reply to
public criticism in Australia that British immigration
was not being sufficiently encouraged by the Australian
Government, the Minister of Immigration wrote a statement to the press in 1958, pointing out some of the
reasons why the British migrants were no longer considered a priority:

> Briefly, we bring to Australia every British mi-
> grant it is possible to bring and gainfully employ.
>
> Not only do we reserve every available berth in
> every ship on the United Kingdom–Australia run
> but – in a world where ships are almost impossible
> to secure – we have managed to charter two excep-
> tionally fine Italian ships for British migrants.
>
> Foreign migrants come to Australia mainly in ship-
> ping provided by the Intergovernmental Committee
> for European Migration. Britain is not a member of
> I.C.E.M. and these ships are not available for her
> nationals. Shipping is a limiting factor in migration
> from the United Kingdom. But even if shipping
> were adequate we could increase the intake of assis-
> ted British migrants substantially only by taking
> many workers for whom there is no great demand in
> Australia.
>
> Giving assisted passages to these low-essential
> types of British migrants would exclude skilled and
> other more useful non-British migrants needed for
> national development and industry.
>
> In other words, to increase British migration to a
> higher percentage, Australia would have to pay more
> to bring out the type of migrant she least needs to
> the exclusion of many foreign migrants with the
> skills she most needs.

Expense has not been overemphasized and we pay approximately four times as much to bring a British migrant here as for a foreign migrant.

We also grant British migrants priorities and concessions in a variety of other ways.

Within the annual 'ceiling' of 115,000, there is no limit placed on the number of British migrants who may come here by paying their own fare although there are, of necessity, limits on other nationals.

Foreign migrants were shipped over in cheaper and less luxurious ships than the British migrants who, in spite of being in more crowded conditions than the ordinary fee-paying passengers, were nevertheless enjoying all the benefits of a six-week cruise. It usually came as a shock to the British migrants when they arrived, after being waited on at dinner and enjoying three course meals on board, to find themselves rubbing shoulders with the other foreign migrants in the far more basic conditions of the hostels. As the British migrants had the advantage of being able to speak the language, they usually arrived with high expectations and then complained loudly when they felt they were being badly treated. They were less amenable than the European refugees and other displaced persons so the Australians often referred to them disparagingly as the 'whingeing Poms'.

It is interesting that it was not the British Government which insisted on the high standard of accommodation on migrant ships but the Australians who wanted to create a good impression on the British passengers to their host country. The Report of the Commonwealth Advisory Committee of 1946 states that:

The amenities so desirable for migrants on a long sea voyage should be provided on all ships. They were noticeably absent in many migrant ships of the past. The Australian standard of comfort would be a favourable impact on the migrant from the moment he stepped on a ship. In ships provided with Australian books and pictures, and screening Australian documentary films with lectures on the Australian way of life, the six weeks' voyage would afford a profitable undergraduate course in Australianism.

These suggestions were taken up by Calwell and all the migrant ships provided some instruction and advice about life in Australia, although this depended a great deal on the dedication and efforts of the ships' welfare officers, some of whom took their responsibilities for educating new immigrants very seriously. Further education in 'Australianism' was provided in the hostels, particularly in areas such as language teaching for foreign migrants and background information about training for jobs and job opportunities, housing, education and facts about the cost of living. There were Good Neighbour Councils, set up by the Government in each State and Territory, to help migrants integrate and to smooth out problems between the newly arrived immigrants and the local people. The Good Neighbour Movement was set up at the first Australian Citizenship Convention in 1950 and depended mostly on voluntary workers. The movement grew rapidly and, as it developed, became responsible for providing a wide range of migrant services. An Australian Information Service publication of 1973 outlines the tasks of the Good Neighbour voluntary work forces:

I) welcome new arrivals and help them to settle smoothly and rapidly into the community;

II) act as advisers to the Government on migrant integration matters and also to act in liaison with the Australian and State Departments of Immigration;

III) maintain and encourage public awareness of the importance of planned immigration to Australia's national development in all its aspects;

IV) encourage the establishment and involvement of appropriate community services and organizations in meeting the needs of migrants;

V) encourage the acceptance of a philosophy among all people in Australia to develop a true spirit of a 'family of a nation' and encourage community development projects towards this end;

VI) provide direct assistance to migrants where existing services are not readily available, including a network of Good Neighbour workers throughout Australia; and

VII) emphasize the importance of non-English-speaking migrants taking full advantage of the many facilities available for learning English. The Councils agreed to take an active part in this work, in co-operation with the authorities concerned, and to provide voluntary tuition to supplement the official programme where necessary.

This kind of voluntary service was also provided by organizations set up by the different churches. One of these was the Catholic Federal Committee for Migration whose active role is described by Father

Meacham, a former chaplain on one of the migrant ships:

The church sponsored Catholic children who went out on the Ten Pound Fare and there were also parish nominations where the parish would sponsor a person or a family. The priest of that parish would arrange accommodation for the immigrants and find suitable work. The church had a loan scheme to help migrants to set themselves up. There was also an International Catholic Migration Committee set up in 1952 which lent out about seventeen million dollars to people coming out to Australia (interest free). Families who did not qualify for assisted passages were given a third to half the cost of their fare over. The Saint Vincent de Paul Society provided furnishings for the houses of newly arrived immigrants and would also arrange for basic provisions to be supplied. Quite a number of parishes provided immigrants with a home where they could stay for up to two years on a very low rent. The church was particularly concerned that families should not be separated on arrival in Australia. Members of the Society would visit the new arrivals and give them food orders for one of their own stores, which also provided clothes and second-hand, reconditioned furniture. Families would be helped in this way until they had managed to set themselves up.

There were also Catholic schools where those who could afford to pay the fees did so and there was a special arrangement for those with large families. The first child you paid for if you could; for the second child there was a ten per cent discount; for the third child a fifty per cent discount and any others went free.

In the early years of the Scheme, there was a bias against Catholics in certain firms and banks. Before the War, the Catholic migrants were mostly Irish from very poor families. For certain white collar jobs, they liked you to come from an established Protestant school. Also the Catholics are never Masons and the Masons were particularly strong in the commercial world. For most jobs it didn't matter what your religion was, as long as you could do the job properly. On the whole, Catholics found it easier to settle than many other groups because there was this supportive Catholic network behind them.

The voluntary services became an important part of the immigration programme, particularly when some of Calwell's successors allowed more than double the intake of yearly immigrants, regardless of his cautions that the country could not absorb more than two per cent of its numbers. Instead of the steady but limited intake of migrants originally planned, the immigrant intake began to go in waves, depending on the state of the Australian economy, the number of migrants available and also the shipping available to take them over. Usually a large migrant intake was followed by a recession and then, when the newly arrived immigrants had become absorbed into the community, and when the Australian economy had picked up and was strong enough to take in more people, another influx would follow. After a wave of new immigrants in 1949 and 1950, which took its toll on the economy, the Government decided to cut its target number from 150,000 to 80,000. It became the general policy to increase and reduce immigrant numbers according to the needs of the Australian economy and to select those who best suited the economic needs of a particular time. To begin with, the Commonwealth Government was most interested in young couples who would produce children. They were often semi-skilled workers who might need further training in Australia or unskilled labourers who could be employed for a number of different jobs. Later, when a large number of immigrants were available from all over Europe, the Australian Government became more specific about the kind of skills that were required, particularly technological skills that were needed for major construction work, like the Snowy River Project.

A Government Report of the early 1970s recommends the following considerations:

1. The maximum possible intake of migrants with particular emphasis on the migration of family groups;

2. That special encouragement be given to those best fitted to assist in national development, with particular emphasis on meeting the needs of rural industry;

3. A vigorous campaign for sponsorships;

4. The chain of migration of relatives already settled in Australia;

5. A more reasonable balance between the sexes;

6. The maximum encouragement of complete industrial undertakings and of people with special and technical skills;

7. That the moral, physical and mental standards of migrants be ensured by sufficient medical examination and screening (discretion to be exercised in special cases of hardship);

8. An increase in the quota of the disabled, aged, refugees and orphans;

9. That permanent residence be granted to certain classes and categories of Asian nationals, viz.:

a) Those already admitted under existing immigration laws and their wives and families;

b) Graduates of Australian universities, technical colleges and institutions;

c) Families, husbands, wives and children of Asians who have been granted Australian citizenship.

The last category represents the biggest change in Australia's immigration policy from its inception. When Calwell first set up his immigration policy he intended to bring in as many British people as possible and a smaller quota of white Europeans but no Asian people. After the threat of the Japanese invasion, Australians became extremely sensitive to the Yellow Peril and any immigrant of Asian origins was automatically disqualified. There had been a White Australia policy long before this; a Government paper produced by the Immigration Reform Group states that:

The origins of the White Australia policy go back as far as the Gold Rushes of the Eighteen Fifties, when the Chinese accounted for about 7 per cent of the Victorian population. In later years the separate colonies took various measures to exclude them, but the demand for 'White Australia' is associated historically with the tide of fervent nationalism that led to Federation.

There were several reasons, some good, some bad, why the demand to exclude 'coloured' immigrants became so intense in the last decades of the nineteenth century. 'Cheap labour' seemed incompatible

IMMIGRATION
AND THE
"WHITE AUSTRALIA" POLICY

by R. DIXON

ASSISTANT SECRETARY
AUSTRALIAN COMMUNIST PARTY

3D

with the social ideal of a fair and reasonable wage standard. On at least one occasion, there had been an attempt to use the Chinese as strike-breakers. It was a time of sharp political and economic conflict between the employers and organized labour, which added to the working man's fears. The Australian Chinese certainly had strong inducements to take any employment they could get, and little sense of solidarity with the Australian workers, who despised them. In the debates in the Federal Parliament on the 1901 Immigration Restriction Act, economic criticism was mingled with attacks on their servility, their alien dress and customs, their frugality, their gambling, and their alleged immorality.

Meanwhile the introduction of Kanaka labour on the Queensland canefields gave rise to fears of a wider importation of cheap indentured labour. The result would have been not merely to lower wages and weaken the new-born Labour movement, but also to make possible the development of a paternalistic, plantation-type society similar to that of the American South. The whole concept was offensive to the egalitarian ideals of Australian nationalism.

The notions of 'racial purity' and 'racial contamination' had been given currency by fashionable theorists in Europe and America. Respect or understanding for Asian civilizations, about which little was known, was hardly increased by the fact that the Chinese and Indian coolies and hawkers whom Australians had seen were mostly drawn from the lower strata of Asian society.

In order not to offend the British Government, which would have resented any open racial discrimination against Asian countries, the Australians introduced the dictation test so that Asians could be excluded for 'language' reasons and not on racial grounds. The test consisted of writing fifty words in a European language of the officer's choice. This so-called dictation test could be used by an immigration or customs officer to disqualify any would-be immigrant, considered undesirable. The Immigration Restriction Act also gave the Federal Government the means to exclude non-Europeans where it was thought necessary for economic reasons or considered that assimilation would be difficult. It was not until 1958 that a new Act, repealing the previous legislation, provided for a new immigration procedure:

> There is no reference to race or nationality; and the dictation test is abolished. Anyone can be admitted if he has an entry permit. But whether the permit is granted is wholly at the discretion of the Minister and his officials. Certain classes of persons will *ipso facto* be refused permits, e.g. persons suffering from prescribed diseases, convicted criminals and persons using forged documents. Otherwise nothing is stated as to the grounds on which permits will be granted.
>
> The Act also provides for temporary permits, which are given to all non-European entrants. This may be cancelled by the Minister 'in his absolute discretion', but a new permit may be granted each time the old one expires.

Although Australia gradually began to accept a wider and wider range of nationalities and the White Australia policy was finally abolished, British emigration continued to be an important part of Australia's immigration programme and, up to the end of the 1950s, was actively encouraged. Only during the period of Australia's economic recession in 1952–3 was immigration reduced on all fronts and the target for British immigrants was limited to 40,000. The vast intake of immigrants in 1949 and 1950 may have been partly to blame for the economic problems that Australia suffered during this recession, besides the decline in wool prices. One of the peak periods for British emigration was in the immediate post-war years; by the late 1950s economic conditions had improved in the UK so people were less interested in emigrating. After the War, there was still food rationing in Britain, though this became progressively less severe. There were Government controls on production and the Minister of Labour had the power to direct workers into essential employment although most people were only too keen to take the jobs that were offered. In spite of the shortage of housing, those who wanted to renovate bombed houses or ones that had been ransacked during the War had to obtain a Government permit to do so and found themselves in a web of time-consuming bureaucracy. Many houses were left derelict for years. The prospect of emigrating to a sunny land, free of those debilitating Government restrictions and where there was an ample supply of food and plenty of work available, must have seemed like a golden opportunity. Most British people also regarded Australia as a safer place to live. After the Suez crisis of 1956–7, there was a sudden new surge of interest in Australia, as there was after the Korean War of 1950–51 when, as a result of an increased expenditure on defence, the British standard of living rose sharply and the world prices of raw materials also went up. Some of the more patriotic

British people looked on emigration as hardly better than desertion during wartime but others, who had suffered years of hardship, felt there was no reason why they should have to endure such conditions in times of peace. There was usually a number of reasons why a British family would decide to emigrate and families would often consider the pros and cons for years before making the final decision to go or, in the end, decide not to go after all. Some couples waited because they had elderly parents to look after and felt the journey would be too long and tiring for them. Others were reluctant to leave their council accommodation, which they might have waited many years to acquire. Quite a number wanted to see how quickly economic conditions in Britain would improve. Sometimes a delay in making a decision made emigrating harder rather than easier. Young couples without children usually found it was much less difficult to find accommodation and get work in Australia than those who had a young family to look after. Nevil Shute, the famous author, also involved in the Australian immigration movement, had some firm words of advice to couples with young families in a speech he gave at the Australian Citizenship Convention in 1959:

In Australia, speaking very generally, wage standards are much higher than in England, but out of his wage the man is expected to buy and own his house. House ownership is normal in Australia; it is not so in England. For myself, I much prefer the Australian way, though it creates enormous difficulties for the would-be British migrant, who living on a lower wage in a rented house has been unable to save up the capital to pay the down-payment on a house on his arrival in Australia.

I am a novelist; I write stories dealing partly with Australia and I get a considerable fan mail from my readers. Four or five times a year I find amongst this mail a letter from a would-be British migrant seeking advice. They come from many walks of life, but an average of the letters might read something like this. 'My wife and I have read all your books and wonder if you can help us. We are worried about the future for our children in England and think while we are young we ought to try it in a newer country. We have three children, ten, seven and four years old. I am thirty-five, and I am a charge-hand machinist with the Rover Company in Coventry. I have written to General-Motors-Holden and I think I could get a job with them all right. We live in a council house and own our own furniture, but we only have about £100 saved up. Would you advise us to try it in Australia?'

My reply is always in the same terms. 'Stay where you are, chum, till the children have grown up. If you come to Australia it may well be three or four years before you can get a house comparable with the one you live in now. Until you do, you will have no home life and you may even have to live apart from your wife and family. Without a home your wife is likely to be miserable and discontented with Australia, and your children will grow up unhappy and undisciplined. Let them grow up in the stable English home that you have made for them where you can influence them and bring them up in the right way. Then let them emigrate when they leave school, if they should want to.' One can give no other advice to a man whose main concern is for the welfare of his family, but in this way I have deterred a number of British families from coming to this country.

There would be little financial risk if the Federal Government were to guarantee the payments on a house to be hire-purchased upon no-down-payment terms by every British family migrant with one child or more, for loss could only be incurred if the house were to stand empty. That this has not been done may be because political reasons make it difficult to favour British families in comparison with young Australians, or it may be for sheer lack of understanding of the problems of migration. The present system, however, imposes far greater hardships on the British family migrant than the young Australian is called upon to bear, and until this matter is tackled I do not think that many good class British family migrants will be attracted to Australia unless considerable unemployment should develop in the United Kingdom. There will always be a certain flow of adventurous young single men coming to Australia from the United Kingdom, but unless Australia embarks upon a policy of attracting the family migrant by offering living conditions comparable with those that he has left from the first day he lands, I think that immigration from the United Kingdom will fall off fairly rapidly. Australia will have to woo the immigrant if she is to fill her spaces with the sort of immigrant she wants.

In spite of advice of this kind, many young couples with children did take the risk and did not realize until they had arrived in Australia how much more difficult

it was for a family with young children. Without sufficient means to put down a deposit on a house they
were unable to buy one. Rental accommodation was
easier to find in Australia and there were less Government restrictions on landlords and tenants, but many
Australian landlords disliked renting flats to families
with young children because they thought that they
would be noisy and would be more likely to make a
mess of the flat. There were some housing associations
which provided flats, first on a rental basis, and later
made them available for tenants to buy, without demanding a large down-payment – but there were long
waiting-lists for this type of accommodation. The kind
of protected Government housing that exists in England did not exist in Australia and Nevil Shute certainly
had a point when he advised families with young children to stay in Britain.

Perhaps it was fortunate that many of the early migrants were ignorant of the pitfalls awaiting them on
their arrival. If they had been more aware, they might
never have set off on the long sea voyage that would
take them to the other side of the world.

2

*T*HE VOYAGE OUT

*M*ost of the boats used to transport mi-grants to their Australian destinations were large, luxury liners converted back from being escort carriers during the War. These conversions took time and ships were scarce, so those in use were filled to capacity. Except in special circumstances (such as honeymoon couples who were occasionally allowed to share a cabin), men and women were divided up and had to sleep in separate cabins. Many families resented being split up and found the six-week voyage in these overcrowded conditions a strain, but others enjoyed the good meals, entertainments and social life on board and looked on the journey as a holiday. They did not have to pay for anything (except for extras like drinks at the bar) and although some missed their fish and chips, others appreciated the cooked breakfasts, three-course luncheons and dinners. As one of the ship's welfare officers recalled:

All the food was fresh every day. The bread was baked daily and if you were served stew one day you wouldn't ever get it the next – that all went over-board. They made sure that no one would ever suffer from food poisoning or anything like that. I once went up to one of the Chief Pursers and asked whether we could cut up some of the cake from the day before for the children's party and he said, 'No, we'll make some special ones, everything goes out.'

Dinner

: —

Veloute Genin

Poached Fillets of Cod, Fines Herbs

Calf's Head, Tyrolienne

Roast Quarter of Lamb, Mint Sauce

Baked and Boiled Potatoes
Green Peas

Roast Duck, Anglaise

Cold Sideboard :

Pressed Beef   **Pork Loaf**

Sultana Pudding
Cream Ices

Dessert

Tourist
s.s. "Otranto"   Tuesday, 27th March, 1951

Sometimes for children's parties they'd make bombe alaskas and the children would start crying out that the pudding was on fire. The chefs were really good chefs, they could turn out all sorts of wonderful pastries. Once every trip – when we crossed the equator – we'd have this buffet on deck and it was beautiful. In the evenings there'd be dancing in the main hall; the cinema, which had a good collection of pictures; then there was the piano in one bar

SHAW   SAVILL   LINE

MENU

Consommé Royale
Poached Fresh Salmon, Cucumber, Batarde
Sweet Corn on the Cob, Melted Butter
Baked York Ham, Madere
Roast Norfolk Turkey, Chipolata
Brussels Sprouts
Browned & Boiled Potatoes

COLD BUFFET

Or Tongue   *Roast Lamb*
Bologna Sausage   *Oxford Brawn*

SALADS

Lettuce   Tomato   Onion   Mixed Salad

DRESSINGS

Roquefort   -   *Thousand Island*

SWEETS
Crème Caramel
Coupe Jacques
Cream Ices

Coffee

where they could go and have a good sing-along; there was plenty to do.

A lot of the passengers had never been on board ship before and many were seasick. Quite a number were also homesick; many had never travelled abroad and they missed their families. The leave-takings before the journey were particularly poignant because most of the migrants believed they would never see their families again:

The passengers' relatives usually came to say goodbye to them at Waterloo, very few came down to Southampton. That was what I was so sad about – they didn't see the ship sail. I suppose some of them couldn't have afforded the fare there and back. There were always a lot of people weeping at Waterloo. Some of the passengers looked completely stunned. You know – 'We've made this big decision and here we are at last – what's going to happen?' They were probably quite frightened.

The welfare officer's job was to help the passengers embark at Southampton, look after their personal needs throughout the journey and answer any queries they might have about life in Australia. She also showed them where to go and what to do on the boat when they first boarded:

The first day out, I'd go down by train from Waterloo and you'd see these people who'd sold their homes, probably sat on the station overnight with children crying. When we got to Southampton there'd be no porters to help anybody, but the Southampton Red Cross ladies were fabulous, they'd meet the train, cope with the children, help the people with their luggage, they did everything to help them embark on the ship. The first day on board ship they'd be settling into their cabins and getting used to the routine.

The routines varied depending on the ship but this welfare officer recalled the timetable on her ship:

From seven-thirty till nine in the morning there was breakfast, then there were two separate sittings for lunch at twelve-thirty and one-thirty [the children had an earlier lunch at around 11.30 and an early evening meal around 5.30], and then there would be two sittings for dinner at seven-thirty and eight-thirty.

After dinner there were the evening's entertainments. There were also special activities arranged for the children. After everyone had settled in, the welfare officer used to brief the parents:

The following day I'd get them all together in the main lounge, give them a talk, tell them what was going to happen and explain that I was going to run a school. I'd ask for volunteers to help [the school was only for one hour a day in the mornings which gave the parents time to do their washing and other things]. I also organized games for the children and I needed volunteers to help with these. I'd try and keep the children occupied from nine in the morning until bedtime so that they didn't wear their parents out. There'd be fancy dress, all sorts of parties for them, the crossing-of-the-line ceremony when we crossed the equator – some of the boys on the ship or some of the fathers would dress up as King Neptune with all his attendants and they'd duck the children in the pool (adults often got a ducking too). There was school from nine till ten, then games, then we'd go to lunch, then there was the nursery where the children could rest in little cots and afterwards the children would sit down and sing 'Old King Cole' etc., and really shout their lungs out.

at the Equator

Then we'd organize a concert and at Christmas we'd get all the little horrors to sing carols and dress them up as angels. The ship always had the most beautiful Christmas trees and they put on a children's party and gave them toys which were probably the best toys most of the children had ever had in their lives.

Not all the welfare officers were such good organizers or so diligent, but many of them, like this one, also tried to educate the parents about their future way of life. She would give them talks about housing in Australia, health, job opportunities, show them films and slide shows about their new country and talk to them about social habits and customs.

I'd have a special get-together for the women and

I Neptunus Rex, do hereby command seafarers wherever ye may be, know ye that on this day, the 27th of March, 1951, ye goode shippe "Otranto," appeared within the limits of Our Royal Domain and

.... *Jill Hall* ....

was duly admitted into the Ancient Order of the Solemn Mysteries of the Deep.

Given under my hand and seal the day and year aforesaid, aboard ye goode shippe "Otranto" of ye Oriente Lyne.

Neptunus Rex,
Ruler of the Raging Main.

"Otranto" crosses the Equator
about 10 p.m.

A certificate was issued to everyone to celebrate crossing the equator

set up a panel with some of the Australian ministers' wives or other women on board who knew Australia well and let them ask us questions. They'd ask all sorts of little things – like the kind of clothes-lines that are used out there or what time of year the weevils get at the raisins. These things sound silly, but for someone coping with a large family they were very important. Often I'd get a migrant who'd returned home and was coming back again to give a talk. I couldn't get a better ambassador for Australia than one of the returnees.

There were usually three ministers on board to give services and counsel migrants – two Protestant and one Catholic. The Protestant ones might be Anglican, Presbyterian or Methodist. Church organizations like the Catholic Federal Committee for Immigration sponsored migrants and provided chaplains. One of these Catholic chaplains on board ship was Father Meacham:

> If there were over 950 migrants on a ship, they usually arranged for there to be three ministers for the Irish, Scottish and English Christians: one Catholic priest and one Church of England, and a Baptist or Presbyterian minister.
>
> The Catholics had the best organization for assisting new immigrants because we had been helping migrants since the Irish came to Australia during the famine. In 1947, when the Assisted Passage Scheme started, we set up the Catholic Federal Committee for Migration. About one in ten migrants were Catholics on the migrant ships, which was more or less the same proportion as the percentage of Catholics in Britain. Besides the chaplains on board ship, there would also be a Catholic chaplain in the hostel. If they were going to stay with friends or relatives, or in a special house, arranged for them by the church, the priest from that parish would usually come down to the ship to greet them. The Catholic Federal Committee for Migration kept in touch with Australia

House and knew of all the Catholics who were emigrating so that the parish priests could be told in advance who was coming out and when. Calwell was keen that the churches should play a part in the Assisted Passage Scheme because he felt that, if the migrants became involved in a parish, they would settle more easily. On the whole that was true.

I went as a Catholic chaplain on two trips in 1950 and 1954. There was a Mass each day and I spent quite a lot of time counselling migrants. There were not usually many problems during the voyage. Most migrants enjoyed themselves very much on their way out.

Some of the ships were just ordinary liners that took a certain number of migrant passengers. These were popular but even then two migrant families on the same ship could react quite differently to the journey. Younger members of the family usually took more part in the social life on board and to them it was often their first taste of independence. They found themselves outside the usual constricting influences of families and local neighbourhoods and were able to go off on their own and make new friends. One couple who took with them a sixteen-year-old daughter, who had been reluctant to leave England and her first steady boyfriend, found that she cheered up enormously on board ship:

Anne loved the journey out here. There were lots of young people on board and she had a very good time. In fact we all did. It was a glorious holiday. We went to Gibraltar, Naples, through the Suez

Canal. We were never treated as migrants on board ship, never. It wasn't just a migrant ship, it was about fifty-fifty. Half those on board were ordinary passengers. None of them even asked us whether we were migrants, we were treated as equals. We made some very good friends on board who we kept up with when we got to Australia.

Another couple who went over on the same boat, the *Fairsea*, but on a different journey (when there were probably only migrant families on board), had far less favourable memories of the voyage:

It was overcrowded and that was a bad start, especially if you had children to look after. Some of the crew were very, very rude — particularly the waiters in the lounges and that and the cleaners — and you know what children are, all running around the corridors screaming and shouting. Some of the wives with three or four young children had a terrible time. But then it was a migrant ship, you couldn't expect it to be five-star accommodation, could you! The food was all right in bulk, but it was a bit slap-handled. There were always dances at night time and there was a film show once about Australia and they showed you the estate housing and all that sort of thing. We were given booklets and everything and there was a chap on the ship who told us what to expect when we came here. We'd had an image in our mind that the voyage was going to be like, you know, a sea cruise — but it was totally different to what we thought. It was much tougher than we expected. The people were all the same type of people — migrant families like us — but from all over England. Some of the children were very rough and ready. There was also some petty thieving – we found my daughter's little teddy bear stashed in this woman's case before we left, but we didn't say anything, we just left it. It was the last day of our voyage and we weren't going to make a fuss. People often found little things missing but then we were all living on top of each other – it was a bit of a cattle ship really.

The welfare officer was used to complaints of this kind and kept a wary eye out for bad behaviour but it must have been hard to keep an eye on so many passengers. On an average ship there were about twelve hundred people and some like the *Fairstar* carried about nineteen hundred. She learnt to take all the complaints in her stride:

There were always some grizzlers on board. On the big ships there'd often be quite a number. People wanting more stopovers, for instance. Also there were always people losing their cases and getting very upset about it. We laid on a lot of things to keep the passengers happy, so they wouldn't be mooching about. There was a library, they could play deck tennis or different games, there were films for the children and every night there was a dance. There were also special nights like Equator Night when the boys would decorate the ship – it was beautifully done. There'd be a Pirate's Night, an Arabian Night, an old-time singing night. There was a couple of chaps in the Purser's Office who organized all these entertainments and they did them really well.

There was considerable tension on board, partly

ON BOARD A PENINSULAR AND ORIENTAL STEAM NAVIGATION COMPANY'S SHIP

Did you put your CLOCKS forward last night?

8.30 a.m.   Cocos Islands (Port Side)

7.15 a.m.   Physical Culture Class on "A" Deck After end

2.15 p.m.   Whist Drive on "B" Deck Forward outside Lounge

4.30 p.m.   Children's visit to the Navigation Bridge

5.00 p.m.   Recorded music to "B" and "E" Decks

9.15 p.m.   Housie Housie in "B" Deck Forward Lounge

9.00 p.m.   Cinema for Lavender Ticket Holders
            "Postcard from Perth" and "Alive & Kicking"

9.00 p.m.   Orchestra Dance on "B" Deck Dance Space

Clocks will be ADVANCED 30 minutes to-night.

————ooooooooo————

Tuesday, 10th March, 1959

because of the close proximity in which all the passengers had to live and partly because many were concerned about their future. They were all facing the unknown and they knew at this stage there was no turning back.

People's hopes and fears would fluctuate. A fitter would come on board at Southampton and next week he was sure he would be a turner, the next week he's the foreman and the next week he's the fitter again. The last week before we got to Australia you could tell that they would be getting a bit nervous.

Besides this general sense of tension, there were sometimes outbreaks of violence but they were rare and the crew took a firm line with any offenders. The welfare officer recalled that:

One night I was woken by a dreadful scream and I came out and found that this difficult chap, Jo, who came from Leeds – he was always threatening to throw his weight around – was threatening to do the doctor in. We always had an Australian or English doctor on board to look after the passengers (he got a free trip out). At two in the morning the doctor had told this Jo and his friends to keep quiet – they had really been whooping it up right beside the cabins. Anyway, we dealt with him and the next morning I really ticked him off good and proper. I told him that I'd written to the Department about him . . . I showed him what I'd written and I said, 'You think you've put one over me, well, have a look at this. That's what's gone in about you. If I could send you back I'd see that you'd go back on somebody else's ship, not mine.' I had to put the wind up him a bit to keep him peaceful because he could have put a knife in someone.

In fact there was little that the Department of Immigration could have done at this stage, once the migrants had been vetted and allowed on board but most migrants were nervous of the kind of reception they would get in Australia so the threat was an effective one.

One ship's steward, who spent from 1950 to 1952 on a migrant ship the *Asturias*, got to know many of the passengers:

Lots had little or no money, not even enough to buy the cheap ship cigarettes. Only a few were fully trained in good trades; quite a lot were semi-skilled or had no skills at all. Most of them did not have any job fixed up for themselves, although the Aussie officials on the boats would help to arrange jobs for them and set them up in hostels where they would be able to find work. Some went to jobs that were very different from what they had done in Britain. I met families in Manchester who had been working in industry who were going off to remote sheep farms, and Scots countrymen who went to work in factories in Sydney. There were also a lot of army personnel who transferred to the Australian forces.

It was always very distressing watching the final farewells when the ship left Southampton. They used to play 'Hearts of Oak' and other traditional old songs over the tannoy and everyone was weeping; a lot of them felt that they would never again see the loved ones they were leaving behind. Australia really was a long way away in those days and it felt almost as if the migrants were going off to a different planet. The types that were prepared to go, especially those with hardly any money, were very enterprising people. It took a lot of guts to leave behind all your home ties, knowing that you'd got hardly anything to fall back on.

The big migrant ships, like the *Asturias*, had a regular itinerary. It was before the Suez crisis so we went from Southampton to Malta, to Port Said, through Suez to Aden, Colombo, Fremantle, Melbourne and Sydney. After Suez, the ships usually went via Cape Town.

It was very crowded on board. We had about 1,200 on the *Asturias*. The men and women were split up in separate cabins so husbands and wives used to go to the upper deck for nightly romancing. The deck watch officers would help them by turning off all the surplus lighting.

The ships were not air-conditioned and were ill-equipped for tropical weather so lots of people slept on the decks. They would lie on blankets and the breeze from the ship would help to keep them cool. Anyone could do that if it was too hot in the cabins and there wasn't any hanky-panky on the main decks.

There were not many entertainments in those days compared to modern cruises. There were film shows, fancy dress, boxing matches set up by members of the crew, but the talents of the crews themselves always amazed me. They would put on wonderful shows for the passengers with short sketches, songs, jokes. Some of the men were kitted out in beautiful drag costumes and there were some really good guitarists and singers among our crew members.

Occasionally we had a funeral on board and these were very sad affairs. After the service the engine speed was reduced, there was total silence and then we'd hear the body hitting the water. Not many died at sea but quite a number were ill during the voyage. There was a ship's hospital and a doctor and nurse on board. Most of the passengers only suffered from minor ailments like stomach upsets or heat-stroke.

A lot of people enjoyed the voyage but there was always a sense of tension, people wondering whether they had taken the right decision. The journey gave them plenty of time to think about it after all the rush of departure. Lots of passengers said they would not go back to Britain, even if they found it hard-going in Australia, because their pride would not let them, but a lot of them worried about how they'd cope when they got there. During my time as a steward, I kept up with a number of passengers after they'd disembarked and I sometimes went to visit them in their homes during stopovers. Quite a lot found it a struggle to begin with but some did very well. If I had my time over again, I'd be one of those Ten Pound adventurers.

Many of the migrants were concerned about the anti-Pom attitudes of Australians that they had heard about from returning migrants or read about in the newspapers. A fair proportion of the questions put to the welfare officer were about the Australians' behaviour towards the British.

They'd hear from returning migrants that the English were called 'Pommies' and 'Pommy Bastards' and I used to say to them, 'It depends on you whether they like you or not. Look at the Australians' eyes when they say things like that, because it can be a term of endearment. It's up to you, it's your personality that will really count. They will like you for yourself. What's in a name?' There was one great big bear of a chap and he came down one day to the office and he said to me, 'Do you know what I'm going to do to the first person who calls me a Pommy Bastard?' So I said, 'No, you Pommy Bastard, what are you going to do? Are you going to flatten me?' and he said, 'No.' So I said, 'Do you think I meant that as something nasty? . . . People can say Pommy and it can mean Prisoner of Old Mother England or that their cheeks are like pomegranates, there's all sorts of explanations. Just watch their eyes. If there's a twinkle you'll know it's a joke. It's up to you to make sure that they accept you, you've got to go half way anyhow.'

In England in the Fifties the term 'bastard' was usually a term of abuse but in Australia it could be used affectionately. British migrants were often resented by Australians because they thought of themselves as coming from a more developed and cultured country and regarded the Australians as rednecks who lived in a provincial backwater. Attitudes such as this did not help to endear them to their new countrymen. Foreign migrants, especially the displaced persons with no home to return to, were usually more adaptable to the Australian way of life.

Some British migrants believed that Australia would

be a sunny outpost of Britain; they never thought of themselves as going to a foreign country. The older ones sometimes found it harder to adapt but this was not always the case. In order that young couples with children should stay in Australia and not return home after the first two years, their elderly relations were often allowed to migrate with them. One family took with them their seventy-year-old grandmother who adapted quickly to life on board ship and to her new life in Australia. The family were amused to find that she soon attracted an admirer on board:

She was a very independent lady and she would go off and talk to people and make friends. There was this little crowd of elderlies and there was one elderly man, quite a nice gentleman, very nicely spoken, who was quite mad about Mum. She was a very attractive old lady. She had beautiful silver white hair and beautiful brown eyes. She'd always been very beautiful. She came to me one day and said, 'Oh, I've got a Johnnie.' She always called them Johnnies because she was born in Nottingham and they always call the fellas Johnnies up there. And when she said this, we all burst out laughing, particularly my eldest daughter, Anne, she thought it was hysterical. Mum said, 'Wherever I turn he's there. He keeps telling me that he likes me. He's a sheep farmer. What do I do with him?' So I said, 'Just play along with it, Mum. Have a bit of fun. You can't come to any harm on a ship.' My mother used to be darting around all over the place after that. Whenever we said, 'He's here,' she'd be off, just like that. When the ship docked at Melbourne, he was on deck shouting 'Elsa, Elsa' (that's my

Mum's name) and she said, 'Oh my gosh, there he
goes again,' and she was off the ship before any of
us. So he came up to me and said, 'Where are you
living?' and I said, 'I don't know,' because I couldn't
tell him, you see. Mum didn't want to be bothered
with him. And I said to her, 'Mum, he's a sheep
farmer, you might have done yourself well there.'
And she said, 'Oh no, I don't want to wash any
more dirty shirts and cook no more breakfasts. No
thank you.' That was her bit of fun on the ship.

The ships provided entertainments specially for the
elderly and grandparents often found a new lease of
life on board, but occasionally the journey proved too
much for them. The welfare officer remembered some
who never arrived at their intended destination:

I got woken up at half past two one morning and
told to come down to the Purser's office and, when I
got there, there was a woman passenger, the Staff
Captain and the Chief Purser and it turned out that
this lady's father had been playing bingo and he'd
won a few nights before and there was great excitement and that night he'd won again and he went
back to his cabin and dropped dead. He was in his
early sixties and I think the strain of coming out plus
all the excitement of the bingo was too much for
him. I had to ask this lady whether she wanted her
father buried at sea or whether she wanted to take
his body to Australia. Of course, she got hysterical
at being asked such a thing, you can just imagine,
and they didn't want the body buried at sea. Then I
had to check that they had enough money in travellers' cheques for whatever they wanted done. I got

in touch with a man in Immigration and it was absolutely fantastic what he did. He arranged for them to disembark at Fremantle and for one of the family to fly over to Wyalla, with the coffin, where the other daughter lived, so that they could all have a proper family funeral. There was a refrigerator in the baggage room which could take a few corpses on board.

On another occasion, an unexpected death provided some macabre humour for the crew:

> Once going northbound on the *Ellinis*, this gentleman died and they put him in the refrigerator in the baggage room. On that trip there was a young officer in charge of the baggage room who was only about twenty-one – he was new to the ship – so the Staff Captain and another officer went down one night and unlocked the lock and moved the crates that this young boy had put against the baggage room door. So the poor kid goes down next day to open the baggage room and he nearly has a seizure. He thought it must have been the ghost of this dead chap who had gone and unlocked it. So anyhow, I came down and said, 'Don't be silly, the dead can't walk.' So I locked it up and helped him shift the crates back in front of the door. The following night the Staff Captain went down and unlocked the door and shifted the crates once again. Poor boy, he was very scared. I told the Staff Captain that he shouldn't tease him like that, the boy was very young.

Sometimes the ships struck storms at sea which frightened the passengers, but they were big, heavy vessels and none of them ever came to grief. The worst that the passengers suffered was a severe bout of seasickness. One lady discovered a cure for this:

> There was an awful gale one night and a lot of people became ill but I met an old colonel who had made friends with me and he was a tough old nut. I was looking a bit green, I think, and he said to me, 'Don't you start,' in his Australian voice. 'You come with me.' And he took me down into the lounge bar and said, 'You must have a sailor's drink.' And I said, 'Oh, well I don't really think I could drink anything.' And he said, 'Oh yes you will.' And he called the steward over and ordered a mixture of half brandy, half port in a little glass and said, 'Now drink that slowly and you'll be down for dinner tonight.'

Most of the passengers enjoyed the stopovers. They were all allowed off the ship during the day but had to return every evening. For many it was their first sight of foreign lands and one nineteen-year-old boy recollected his mother's first reaction to the local Egyptian people:

> I remember when we docked at Port Said – it was the middle of the night – something woke my mother up and she went up on deck to see what was happening and came rushing back down again and woke us all up, saying, 'Come and see – upstairs, on deck – there's crawling with wogs!' They turned out to be sales people selling their wares and they'd set their little stalls up on the deck. Most of us hadn't been out of England and we were very surprised to see these people coming out on little boats and climbing

up on rope ladders onto the deck where they set up a sort of little bazaar.

A significant number of couples emigrated in their late thirties or early forties, so there were usually quite a few teenagers on board. Sixteen-year-old Anne recalled:

I soon made friends on the boat. I met a New Zealand girl, Annette, and she was about the same age as I was. She'd been sort of upheavalled from New Zealand to do this twelve months' trip around Europe and England and she hadn't wanted to go. I think I must have met her one night at dinner because I was old enough to go to dinner with my parents . . . and she introduced me to others who were our kind of age on the boat and we had a fabulous time. We both made our conquests. Terry, the bedroom steward, fell violently in love with me. I really didn't take much notice of him to begin with. There were lots of young ones on the boat and I was generally just having a damn good time. I hadn't ever experienced anything like that and I was just so naive as to what was going on, whereas some of the others had been on cruises before. There was Marilyn who'd been in boarding-school in England, very forward girl she was, and Annette and I got really matey with her. She met up with some real wild boys . . . There was all these dances and parties. And I shared a cabin with Gran. It was all a new experience for me, unlike Marilyn. She was an old hand at these cruises.

John, who went out as a teenager on the *Fairsky*,

found that there were about sixty teenagers on his voyage:

All the teenagers on board went off with their own peer groups. I was chasing girls like crazy. I had several shipboard romances . . . but they were all very light-hearted. I kept up with one girl I met on board for about six months after I arrived. Another one went to a hostel in Sydney and wrote to tell me how dreadful the conditions were there.

In spite of the talks, the shows, educational booklets and even selections of Australian magazines and newspapers to give the migrants a balanced view of the Australian way of life, some of the passengers still harboured some strange preconceptions about their new country. According to the welfare officer:

We used to have to tell them that the kangaroos would not be jumping down the main street to greet them. One trip a silly American chap got on and he had white socks, white shorts, white shirt and a hat like the diggers used to wear. He had photos of aborigines and a couple of elderly ladies came up to me and said, 'You know that man, he's showing us photos of the natives and he says they'll all be there to greet us.' I said to them, 'Yes, the natives will be there but look at me, am I that colour? The ladies will be there with their warpaint on – lipstick, rouge – you wait till you see them, they're not black, they're white like you.' They were really scared stiff that there was going to be nothing but hordes of aborigines.

One couple on their first sighting of the Australian

FOR YOUR LEISURE

The beautiful Lounges on both
SOUTHERN CROSS and
NORTHERN STAR, with their deep
armchairs and settees, are places
of quiet relaxation during the day,
but also the centres of social
activity in the evening.

THE NURSERY

For the tiny tots there is a
playroom and the regular attention
of qualified personnel. There are
other children to meet, as well as a
bewildering number of toys and
lots of exciting games to play.

SHALL WE DANCE?

The Cinema Lounge on SOUTHERN CROSS or NORTHERN STAR is one of the most
popular gathering places in the evenings. Here you will see the latest films, or listen to a concert
by the Ship's Orchestra, or enjoy all sorts of impromptu entertainment. The beautifully
sprung floor and subtle lighting persuade all ages that their dancing years are by no means over
when an informal or formal dance has been arranged for your pleasure.

TEENAGERS THIS WAY

Teenagers as well have their own "den"... a recreation room in which they can work off
"steam". There's table-tennis, a record player with plenty of "pop" discs, and impromptu
dancing to end the day before they take, perhaps, one more "coke" for the road!

OTHER AMENITIES

It will be appreciated that with more than a thousand passengers on board, a bewildering variety of tastes must be catered for.
In addition to the more obvious attractions already mentioned, the following amenities will doubtless be of interest.
On each Sunday morning throughout the voyage, a religious service is held in the Cinema Lounge, whilst facilities are
available for Communion Service to be held for all denominations. There is a quiet Writing Room, as well as a well-stocked
Library with books to suit all tastes. The Ship's Laundry has all the necessary ironing equipment for those who wish to press or
freshen up dresses, etc. There are Ladies' and Gentlemen's Hairdressing Salons, and by no means least, there is the
Ship's Shop where you can buy everything from a box of chocolates to the latest camera. The Ship's Doctors have under their
control a fully-equipped Hospital with a qualified Nursing Staff.

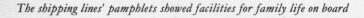

The shipping lines' pamphlets showed facilities for family life on board

coastline happened to pass another of the liners on its return journey:

> When we were approaching Australia, the Captain gave it out over the tannoy that the *Fairsky* was going to pass us on its way back to England, so everybody was up on deck waving and all that and the people on the *Fairsky* were shouting, 'Go back, you blighters, go back.' Those were all the people who had been there for two years and were returning to England and we said to ourselves, 'Oh my God, and that's before we even get there, what are we going to find?'

3

ARRIVAL

*M*ost of the new arrivals were feeling anxious by the time they reached their destination. The first to arrive were those disembarking at Fremantle, which in those days was just a bare wharf with a few big sheds and some railway lines. It was a bleak and not particularly welcoming place to land, but many of the passengers were cheered by the warm weather. One woman from the north of England remembered her surprise at finding out how blue the sky was:

> I thought, 'Oh, brightness, beautiful light.' As my daughter came down the ship she said, 'Oh, Mummy, look at the blue in the sky!' You know England, especially in the north, for nine months of the year it's covered with grey mist. You see, we didn't know any other, we'd lived there all of our lives.

The families who were staying with relations were usually sure of a warm welcome, although tensions might develop later when the British families found themselves living in close quarters with Australian relations they did not know well, if at all. Families with no relatives or other contacts had to go to Government hostels. At the start of the Scheme, everyone who went out had to have a friend or relative who would nominate them. By 1950 the Australian Government had introduced a new immigration scheme under which workers in a wide range of occupations, and their families, could be nominated by the Australian Government and travel out on the Ten Pound Scheme as Commonwealth nominees. A family of Commonwealth nominees who arrived at Melbourne were horrified to find that their hostel accommodation was very different from the life they had led on board ship. Their seventeen-year-old daughter remembers her first sight of Melbourne harbour:

When we arrived at Port Melbourne it was pouring with rain and there were all these wharfies with their singlets and their hankies tied on their heads standing along the wharf and Janet and I just looked at each other and said to Dad, 'Are these all the wonderful bronze Australians you brought us out to meet?' And he didn't think that was very funny at all. Then it was upsetting because I had to say goodbye to Jane and all my friends on the boat and there was a bus there to meet all the migrants; and we were taken to the exhibition building, that was our first reception in Australia and it was a dreadful place. We were all herded into this great hall. And there were these people talking in really strong Australian accents and I didn't like it at all. We spent the night there at the exhibition building and next day we were all put in buses and taken to all these various hostels. And when we got out of the bus at the hostel and saw all these huts we felt we'd arrived at some sort of concentration camp. At the gates we were issued with a knife, a fork, a spoon and a mug, you know, just like a concentration camp, and Gran said, 'I wonder when they'll tattoo us.' She was very good like that, always making jokes. I got

'They're spending more money on migrant hostels — has the price of barbed wire gone up?'

on very well with my Gran and it was a great help having her all through that time. After all we'd been told about this wonderful new country at Australia House, we couldn't believe it when we arrived to find this concentration camp. And the hut was divided long-ways so you could hear everything that was going on the whole length of the hut and of course there were all sorts of foreigners there. And you couldn't do any cooking in the hut, so they told you, you couldn't have any animals, you couldn't do this and you couldn't do that.

They found themselves sharing with immigrants of many different nationalities and this introduction to new cultures, especially as far as the food was concerned, was another unwelcome surprise:

We had to eat in a big mess room, a canteen, and there was a Hungarian cook who made this goulash, real garbage. We just couldn't hack it, just couldn't eat the food. And so good old Mum goes over one day and asks him if he could cook something that we all loved, which was egg and chips, being Poms of course. And they didn't know how to cook that, so Mum cooked it one day for them. I thought the whole hostel was a dreadful place and I really wondered what Mum and Dad thought they were doing. I began to think I'd be spending the rest of my days in this tin hut thing.

One of the problems with the hostels was that many were situated at some distance from the big cities, so newly arrived immigrants seeking work were dependent on getting a bus into town to attend job interviews, and public transport in Australia, particularly outside the city centres, has never been good. Buses would only go infrequently (sometimes they would only go once or twice a week and occasionally there were no public bus services).

Many of the new arrivals expected that jobs were going to be automatically provided for them and they were surprised to discover they had to go and find one (usually by looking through the advertisements in local papers). One of the few hostel services approved of by most of the young couples was the baby-minding centre which looked after young children and left both parents free to find work. In order to earn enough to be able to put down a deposit on a house, most families were glad to have two earners. Mortgages were not hard to get and the terms were much more favourable than those in Britain where few blue-collar workers could afford to buy a house. The biggest hurdle was getting the necessary capital together for the deposit. Flats were also more easily available but rents in the big cities were quite high and couples with young children sometimes had difficulty in getting a flat.

One couple, who came out with four children, stayed on at the hostel because of the child-minding centre until they were both well established in jobs and could get a flat. But they found it a difficult time and the noise at the hostel was one of the worst drawbacks:

> The only really good thing about the hostel was the child-minding centre . . . it meant that my wife, Olive, could work. The centre provided excellent care for the kids. It was quite cheap, too, and if we'd moved out of the hostel we would have had to pay about five to ten pounds a week to have our youngest one looked after and that was an awful lot of money in those days. It meant our child was looked after from seven in the morning until about five in the evening, which fitted in very well with Olive's job. She got a job in a factory doing assembly work. It was her first job since having the children. I was on nights, so I was able to keep an eye on the children till Olive came back from work. I couldn't sleep much in the hostel. I was lucky if I got four hours of sleep in a day. In the summer time, with the Nissen huts being unlined, it was very, very hot. You could have fried an egg on them. After one woman's baby died from the heat, they lined the walls of the huts which made a bit of difference. In the winter they could also be very cold. The meals were quite plenti-ful. We ate in a big canteen and the kids were fed well at the child-minding centre. Sometimes tensions blew up at the hostel and people would throw food at the catering manager or something like that. The frustrations of the place used to get to people. The

food was very institutionalized and my wife hated it. In the end she bought an electric frying pan and cooked us up some meals in secret.

There was a Scots family next door to us and they had a television which they used to have on at full volume, so you can imagine what the noise was like. One of the first things that people bought was a television. Then there was another woman who used to shout these terrible swear words the whole time and we were worried the children would pick them up. As soon as we could afford it, we bought a car and went out at weekends and spent as little time in the hostel as possible.

One family of ten, two parents and eight children, who all came out together, took their own precautions to supply themselves with alternative accommodation: one of the sons said that his father

had organized to take out a great big tarpaulin tent – it was enormous, in a huge wooden box. The idea was that we would have something to live in if we couldn't find anything else. I thought it was rather clever at the time. Everyone tried to persuade him not to take it but he insisted. In the end we never used it because my older brother, who had gone out before the rest of us, had fixed up a flat for us.

Those who went to stay with relations often had a more comfortable time, but they faced other difficulties. One couple and their two children spent four months with the husband's relations and found that family tensions soon built up and the wife did not enjoy being ordered around by her mother-in-law:

My advice to anyone coming out here is never to stay with relatives. They had a very nice house and all that – brick and tile, detached. Arthur's sister and her husband had bought it. Her husband was a returned soldier from the Australian army, so there was Cathleen, her husband and three children and the two of us and our two children and my mother-in-law, who was a real bitch, so interfering. She wanted me to get a job and Arthur to get a job straight away and then hand over the money to her so that she could run the house, but I wasn't going to have any of that.

She also found it difficult to adapt to the easy-going Australian life-style:

The way of life is totally different out here. I used to look on with amazement. Arthur's sister, for instance, she was English and yet she'd got in with the real Australian way of living – casual, off-hand, they don't live by the clock. They eat when they want to, drink when they want to, and do what they want on the spur of the moment. If they wanted to hop on a bus into town, they'd go, whereas we more or less plan our lives, we always have done. And Christmas Day, it was the funniest thing I've ever encountered. On Christmas morning we all got up and the front door was open and this table was set up with only nuts, crisps, pretzels, and that sort of thing and I thought, 'That's not going to be our Christmas dinner, surely not.' And then I discovered that the whole of Christmas Day it was open house and all their friends turned up at different times with a couple of bottles. One group would turn up and sit and have beers and all the rest of it and then they'd go off and another lot comes. Well, this went on all day and I was beginning to get really worked up because I'd bought this leg of pork and there were no signs of it being put in the oven. I mean, we couldn't live on nuts and crisps and things all day long. So I said to Cathleen, 'Cathleen, should I put the leg of pork in the oven?' And of course she was half gone too, she'd been sitting with all these friends drinking beer or what we call plonk, so I lit the oven up and do you know what time we had Christmas dinner? Eleven o'clock at night. That was my first Christmas experience here and I said to myself: 'Mind I'll take damn good care that it'll never happen again, because as soon as the holiday's over, I'm out and I'm renting a house and I'll have my next Christmas in my own place.'

One of the problems for single people who got their own accommodation was loneliness. One boy of nineteen, who came over with his family, managed to get a job immediately and found that he was at last independent of a domineering father and could leave home:

By the time we'd got to Australia the youngest of us was sixteen and we all got jobs straight away. My father was fifty-two then, and, with all eight of us working and on comparatively good pay, he decided he wouldn't have to work any longer. I felt very indignant about this and eventually I said I was going to leave home. Father was furious and we had a real stand-up fight. I was the only one who had stood up to him. The others were too afraid. I packed my clothes, got into a taxi and moved into a friend's

1. December 1945: A young ex-WAAF and her Warrant Officer husband make their first application to emigrate.

2. 1945: A Commonwealth of Australia window display attracts servicemen who are interested in emigration.

3. 1951: A sixteen year old on the Big Brother Youth Emigration
Scheme bids farewell to his Birmingham family. He will be going to
live on a sheep and cattle farm.

4. Belfast, 1960: A particularly large family who have been scheduled
to emigrate.

5. December 1952: Seven of a group of forty boys from the Big
Brother Scheme shake hands with one of the Scheme organizers at
Australia House. These sixteen to eighteen year olds from Scotland
and Shropshire will be settling in New South Wales, some on farms,
some in towns.

6. 1951: Emigrants to Australia give their reasons for leaving Britain. In this period at least two thousand inquiries per week were received in the Migration Department of Australia House, London.

7. 1955: Youthful emigrants on their way to Southampton to board the *Strathaird*.

8. 1949: The Eayrs family from Islington, bound for Sydney.

9. Waterloo Station, 1967: The Hogan family from Liverpool, bound for Fremantle.

10. 1950: A nine-year-old girl, bound for Melbourne, tends to her doll.

11. 1951: Emigrants line the rails of the Orient liner *Oronsay*.

12. The Orient Line R M S *Otranto*.

13. June 1954: Emigrants on the Assisted Passage Scheme arrive in
Australia.

14. A new arrival to Australia in his rudimentary, but personalized, living-quarters.

15. 1954: Cramped accommodation for a family of new Australians.

16. December 1948: Washing up at the Migrant Reception and Training Centre, Bathurst, New South Wales.

17. A drawing lesson at the Bathurst Reception Centre kindergarten.

18. 1954: Migrants who have
formed a Cooperative Building
Society at work on a house.

19. Migrant children among
their pre-fabricated homes.

20. The makeshift caravan homes of some migrants.

21. Migrant J. R. Holt (*right*) has a drink with an Australian friend.

22. A young Ten Pound Pom who came out for a two year 'holiday'.

23. The Bathurst Migrant Reception Centre store.

24. Fred Pilkington, a civil engineering contractor, who persuaded all his firm's employees to emigrate with him. The equipment shown here was also shipped from Britain to Australia.

25. The wife and son of a Pilkington employee, also bound for Australia.

26. The Cassie family from Scotland, who came on the Bring-out-a-Briton Scheme, enjoying a meal in their modern kitchen on arrival in Melbourne.

27. The same family in their 5oft swimming-pool watched by Mr and Mrs Tresise who provided high standard homes for migrants on their Melbourne property.

THE IMPACT
OF IMMIGRATION

Issued by the

COMMONWEALTH BANK OF AUSTRALIA

October, 1950

Migrants working on the Warragamba Dam site near Sydney, N.S.W.
Australian Official Photograph.

28. The impact of immigration: Migrants working on the Warragamba
Dam, New South Wales.

place. For six years I didn't meet the family; it was a rift that took a long time to heal.

I felt a terrible sense of isolation when I got a flat and was on my own. I'd only been in Melbourne a year when I left home. I used to go down to the docks with other English migrants to see the English ships leaving. It was a very emotional affair – watching the boats leaving for the homeland. We'd all get very homesick and go and reminisce about our times in England over a drink.

One of the happiest new arrivals was a young nurse in her twenties who went to share a flat with two other nurses who had gone out to Australia a year before her and already had a good social life.

The day after I arrived I was given a 'Welcome to Australia' party . . . the man who later became my husband and a friend of his came round to the flat to meet me the day before so that I would know a few people before the party. My husband-to-be was a close friend of the other girl in the flat, Gina, but they were more like friends than boyfriend and girlfriend. To begin with, we all went round as a crowd. We were on night-shift so it was very difficult, the only time we could really go out was at the weekends. We'd go to barbecues or the cinema or the beach. I arrived in October and in February I went on holiday with Michael and two of his friends and two children. We went up to Lake Caffey. We'd only started going out seriously together a few weeks before that. To begin with I wasn't terribly interested. I suppose by about Christmas time we were going around a lot together and shortly after this

holiday we decided to get married. It seemed to be a
very natural thing. We just grew together. The holiday went very well. We took it in turns to take care
of the children and we went swimming and fishing
and sight-seeing. I needed that holiday to sort myself
out. I had to think where I was going and what was
going to happen.

Her relationship with Michael, who had an Australian mother and an English father and had gone to
settle in Australia when he was twenty-one, meant that
her open-ended visit, during which she had hoped to
combine temporary nursing jobs with travelling
around the country, now took on a new aspect:

. . . I had to come back and sort out with the girls
in the flat whether or not we were going down to
Darwin which we'd planned to do. Actually, it was
just Gina and I because in the meantime the other
girl in the flat had become engaged. I decided there
was no point my making up my mind until we'd
worked out exactly what we were going to do –
whether or not we were going to go to Darwin first.
In the end we decided not to go because I wasn't
properly qualified to do midwifery over here and
that's what I would have done in Darwin. I'd only
done six months of the hospital part of my midwifery
– in England you only do six months in hospital, six
months on the district, riding around on a bicycle –
but here you have to do a whole year in hospital so,
unless I went back to hospital and did a full year in
obstetrics, there was no point in going. It was odd
because nothing worked out the way I'd planned
but when I got engaged to Michael it seemed as

though everything was fitting into a pattern, as if it was meant to happen. My whole life has been like that – things seem to have just fitted in like bits in a puzzle.

She did not have any qualms about staying in Australia for good and, at the time, felt no sense of homesickness:

I wasn't bothered by the idea of settling in Australia. I thought it was a beautiful country and I didn't mind being apart from my family. I was used to being on my own and doing my own thing. Also, I'd got marvellous friends over here. It just felt like another home to me; it never felt like a foreign country. I never had any desire to go back to England until my daughter was nearly five. Then I just woke up one day and I felt so homesick. That was seventeen years after I'd arrived! I had corresponded frequently with my friends and family so I'd kept up my ties with England. I don't know why I suddenly felt homesick then – there wasn't anything wrong with my marriage or anything like that. It might have been that I had two children and I suddenly realized that my mother might never see them and, if anything happened to her, I wouldn't have seen her. Also, I missed my English friends. I was much closer to my friends than my family in many ways. When I told my husband, he said that I should go back and take my daughter. I had this dreadful feeling that I probably wouldn't want to come back to Australia. You know, I felt that homesick. My husband kept very cool about it all. He never appeared to be worried about my wanting to go home. So we made all the arrangements and when I arrived in England I told these very close friends of mine – a husband and wife – who came to meet me at the airport, 'Look, I've got this awful feeling I don't want to go back. I really feel very homesick.' And they said, 'Wait till you come home and we'll show you what's happened and you'll want to go back.' So they took me back to Leicester that night. We had dinner and then they took me around all the beautiful parts of town that I loved and it had all changed. I think I'd probably changed too.

Many homesick British Poms had much the same experience of returning to a well-loved place. It was no longer the place they once knew and they realized that it was not only the place which had changed, their whole outlook had changed as well. This married woman realized she was no longer the same person as the young nurse who had left England seventeen years before:

I'd quietened down. I used to spend my time dashing here and dashing there. Also I'd got used to a different life-style, much more financial independence and a freer sort of life. You can do a lot more in Australia because the weather's so beautiful. For nine months of the year, almost, you can live out of doors. My friends lived in Leicester and my family lived in Yorkshire so I'd gone to Leicester first and then I went up to see my family.

My father was dead. He'd died when I was twenty. He was a wharfie, a dock labourer. My mother re-married after he died. She married a chappie who was blind and she moved from our house to his so that broke up our family somewhat. His house was much smaller so we couldn't all live at home. It hadn't worried me because I was living away from home already. It didn't upset any of us particularly because a lot of us had already left home. I remember I minded at the time because my mother had had a very hard life and I felt she was needing someone to look after her – my father had had asthma and needed a lot of looking after and she had had seven children – but her second marriage has been a very happy one. Now they're both blind. I sometimes feel guilty that I'm not able to be there and care for her, but being one of a large family, I know the others are looking after her. I would have felt much more guilty if I'd been the only one. Also everyone has their own lives to lead and I have two children and a husband to care for.

My daughter felt smothered by all these unknown relatives she'd never met before. My husband is an only child so she wasn't used to having so many relatives and I think she found it quite hard to cope with. She was keen to get back home. I realized the first night I arrived in England that it was no longer my home either. Australia was my home.

Quite a number who went out on the Ten Pound Fare returned home, usually quite soon after their two years were up, and many of them found themselves disillusioned with England once they arrived. One woman who returned with her husband and small daughter, leaving her grown-up son in Australia, said:

> . . . there's not a thing in the world you can do to stop feeling homesick. You've got to get it out of your system. So I had to go back, but once I got to

England and I got off the ship at Tilbury, it was raining and drizzling, it was absolutely miserable and when I got on the train and looked out of the window I started to cry and the little one started to cry and I said to Arthur, 'Have we done the right thing?' Once we got to England I knew we would return to Australia.

Occasionally, those going out to Australia a second time were given another Ten Pound Fare on the basis that those who had returned and were disillusioned were usually determined to settle in Australia for good the second time around. Many young people who went out the first time because they thought it would be a good way to see the world and have a two-year working holiday (during which they could earn enough for their return fare) often returned to England and found that life in Australia had suited them better, so they would go out again and settle. One young couple with no children had enjoyed life in Melbourne and later returned with two young children to settle in Australia. Unlike many English migrants, they never wanted to think of themselves as Australians and remained firmly British:

If you're offered a trip halfway round the world for ten pounds you'd be a fool not to take it. That's the way I looked at it. Ten pounds was only about a week's wage for a skilled working man. I didn't come out here to settle; I just came out of a spirit of adventure and because I wanted to travel. One of the reasons that I came was that I'd done two years' National Service and I'd spent a year overseas and that gives you a taste for going to new places.

Initially I only came out here for the two years and

after that I went straight back to England. Why I'm here now is not for the same reason that I first came out. I came out under my own steam the second time because by then I'd come up against all the frustrations of Britain in the Sixties and I thought I'd stand a better chance over here.

When we first arrived in Melbourne I only spent a couple of nights in a hostel and then I got out. I got a factory job which I saw advertised in a newspaper and we rented a flat almost straight away. For young marrieds like us with no dependants it wasn't at all difficult to achieve a reasonable living standard quite quickly but couples with children often found themselves stranded in hostels for months.

We soon made friends. Our social life centred round a soccer club. That gave us a social group but we had other Australian and English friends outside the club as well. It's important to join a club in Australia, it gives a focus to your life. The soccer club had regular training evenings; we played games at weekends and there were lots of social functions which my wife came along to. I never encountered any serious anti-Pom feeling. At the soccer club all they really cared about was whether you were a good player. I've never tried to be anything but English and I've never acquired an Australian accent or anything like that. I haven't found that being a Pom affected my work or social life. I've no desire to totally assimilate into this society, I like living in Australia but I've no wish to be an Australian.

On their second visit the young family had hoped to settle in Sydney but were unable to find suitable accommodation:

I brought some savings with me when I came over for the second time. I came back with my wife and young children and we went to Sydney, not Melbourne, because we had intended going up to Queensland to explore that part of the country. British Rail lost all our baggage so when we arrived in Sydney we only had our cabin baggage. We had a stopover in Perth on our way to Sydney and had a look round it. When we got to Sydney we found it was very difficult to rent decent accommodation as we had young children. I was getting more and more fed up with finding somewhere to live and I came back in one of these gloomy moods one day and my wife said, 'Why can't we go back to that nice little place, Perth?' It's half a continent away from Sydney but I just said, 'Right, we will.' And next day we flew back to Perth, knowing nobody there but feeling it might make us all happier, and that was it. The accommodation problems were just as bad in Perth. Nearly all the flats advertised stated 'No dogs, no cats, no children'. Children and pets were considered messy. [It seems a strange attitude for a country that was desperately trying to get its population up!] Eventually we found a flat but it was pretty grotty.

I got a job immediately in sales. My wife didn't work to begin with; she was looking after the children. One thing that struck us when we came to Perth was that lots of people here have never been to any other capital city in Australia. The distances are so vast, it's like going to another country. It's also very expensive going long distances if you've got young children and can't live rough. For our family holidays we now go to the south-west corner of Western Australia, there's some beautiful country up there.'

January 1952

AUSTRALIA
and your future

1952

The distances between cities in Australia (there are about two thousand miles between Perth and Sydney) often came as a shock to the newly arrived British Poms. The Australian expression 'just down the road' could mean any distance, and many Australians would happily make a journey of two or three hundred miles to see some friends for lunch at a weekend. One young man who went to Melbourne tried to continue seeing a girl he had met on the boat who lived in a city north of Melbourne called Shepperton:

> The girl I kept up with lived in Shepperton in Victoria and she asked me over for dinner. I set off, never thinking it would be further than ten or twenty miles away – it turned out to be nearer one hundred and twenty miles! It took me hours to get there and at ten o'clock I set off back again. It didn't encourage me to go on with the relationship.

He came out with the rest of his family when he was twenty and, as he was an apprentice glazier in England, he continued to work in the glass trade:

> . . . it came as a shock to me that my apprenticeship didn't count for much in Australia, they were really only interested in work experience. But I managed to get work and I got on well with my Australian workmates. They were a pretty rugged lot . . . When the Australians first began calling me a 'Pommy bastard' I didn't realize it was just a joke and a sign of acceptance. I was deeply hurt. I never bothered to discuss it, so I didn't find out for ages that I hadn't been insulted. I just kept away from Australians after that. I also didn't understand some

of the Australian slang; like 'he's crook today', I discovered meant 'he's sick today', but I didn't want to show my ignorance so I'd ask the other British migrants.

The first day at work they sent me off with a guy and at ten in the morning he said, 'It's smoko time,' so I lit up a cigarette but he got out his thermos of tea and sandwiches. I thought 'smoko' meant smoking but it refers to the fire, going back to the days when you lit a fire and put the billy can on it to have a cup of tea . . .

When I first arrived I dressed much more formally than the Aussie boys. The day I went for my first job interview I put on this suit because in England you always went to an interview in a suit and it was one hundred and four degrees Fahrenheit and I had to walk along a beach to the interview where everyone was sunbathing. I'd been told the interview was 'just down the road' and found I was in for a two-mile walk. When I arrived for the interview, all the men at work — even the bosses — were in shorts, short-sleeved shirts and thong sandals. I was dressed in an Italian suit, winkle-pickers, a tie and a white shirt and I felt an absolute idiot.

In the cities there were a lot of immigrants, so there was usually a more tolerant attitude towards the British Poms than there was in the country. One middle-aged couple who got a job running a working men's club in the outback of Western Australia found they were not only up against primitive conditions and a far tougher way of life than they were used to, they were also faced at first with a hostile community who disliked the British:

When we first arrived here there was a lot of anti-Pom feeling. We were outsiders there. The first time we went to the club, we cleaned the place out a bit because it was filthy and when the first customers arrived they said, 'Bloody Poms,' so I said, 'Yes, we are bloody Poms. Australians applied for this job but they wouldn't take it because the place was too filthy.' After we'd been there a while they began to respect us but we always felt like outsiders. We were paid seventy dollars a week between us and they gave us this hut to live in.

It was very primitive. I had to get a saw and cut a hole into the bloody bedroom. I felt sorry for some of the other migrants. There was this London family – middle-class, well-spoken – and they were given a wooden shack and had to carry bits of wood up from the mill to sit on. The husband was labouring at the mill. They all went back to England once the two years was up. Then there was this Taffy, a Welsh-man, and he had six children and she was going to have another one and they arrived to find this wooden hut with virtually nothing in it. I felt very sorry for them.

We found the country Australians very brash, casual and bad-mannered. That's how most of them are. The reason why there was this settlement up there was for labouring in the mills, timber mills, that's why they had all this migrant labour . . .

. . . We never had any bad scandals up there except for this fellow, Jimmy, the clerk at the mill. He used to chat up my daughter and she was only eleven then. She was very pretty but only a kid and this fellow was about thirty and he wasn't chatting her up casual-like, he was hoping to get her into bed. I soon straightened him out, don't you worry.

You see on Friday night I had to lock her in by herself. The house was just up at the back but the men had to go past our house to go to the toilet. But, before I locked her into the house, she used to sit out on the front steps and sometimes she'd chop the wood and the men would pass her on the way to the toilet. And apparently this Jimmy, he would come up to her and feel her all over and she said, 'I'll tell my Dad,' but he said to her, 'Don't you dare to say anything.' But she told me, so I said, 'Right.' When he comes into the bar, I said to him, 'You keep away from my daughter. I'll stick a knife in you if you ever speak to her again, let alone touch her.' He said, 'I didn't mean any harm.' So I says to him, 'Just being with her and suggesting anything to her, that's enough for me. That kid's only eleven and you've got six kids of your own. I'll get you expelled from this club. I'll tell the Committee and I'll tell Jock Tamms.' Tamms was his employer at the mill. After that this man Jimmy never touched her. He was frightened he'd get the sack . . .

We left the club when my daughter was twelve because of her education. We went back to Fremantle and she went to John Curtin High School. She's a computer operator now for an American oil company. She's got a good job.

For most British Poms, the first two years were usually the most difficult and testing. Coping with a strange culture and trying to establish a home, a job and often caring for a young family meant that many new settlers were facing up to problems they had never had to deal with in Britain. They also had to come to terms with the loss of their families and friends and overcome a sense of homesickness, which some felt so strongly it seemed to them almost like an illness. Those who survived the early years best were the ones with the most realistic expectations who were good at adapting to unexpected circumstances, and were able to work as a team. When the two years were up, the less adaptable often returned home disillusioned; but the others usually found that they were better able to cope and more independent, and life usually became easier once they had settled into a home and a job. As one young husband, who went to live in Perth with his wife and two children, said:

> We both suffered from a general feeling of frustration because of lack of funds in those first years. When you've no family to fall back on, it means you're totally reliant on each other as a unit. If you get into a fix, there's nowhere to go. My wife became more independent because she couldn't even talk to her mother on the phone and there was no one to help her care for the children. In a way this was quite character-building. Before the end of the first three years we had bought ourselves a house and after that time we really felt we had come to grips with the place and were able to have a reasonable way of life again. The price of houses is much lower in Perth than in Sydney or Melbourne and it's easier to borrow money in Australia (at least it was then). We bought a plot of land and had our house built on it – the whole thing took about five months. I was a sales manager by then and my wife had a job in PR working for a retail store. We had another child as well – a totally Australian one!

When you've no family, your friends are very important. For instance, there were times when we were broke, absolutely broke, and we'd get together and have a laugh about it with friends. Of course you knew you'd be getting your wages at the end of the week or whenever but there were times when we literally didn't have a cent. Our closest friends are an Australian couple we met when we first came to Perth and I remember having a real laugh with them about only having one cent in the world. If we were really stuck for cash they would always help us out.

As a husband and wife we learnt to be very supportive of each other. When one of us was down we had to learn to pick each other up and say, 'Come on, let's go out and have a drink,' and that sort of thing. My wife became a much stronger character as a result of this and she's also the one who's kept us emotionally on an even keel.

It was not necessarily the younger people who were the most adaptable, although they usually found it easier to cope because the middle-aged couples tended to have had a more established life-style. One widow of fifty who came out on her own to join her married son in Australia found the challenge of a new life was a wonderful experience. After spending years meeting the needs of a demanding husband and mother-in-law, she suddenly found herself free to travel and do as she liked:

I was twenty when I married and I'd been living at home till then. My husband was eleven years older than me and he treated me like a child, he was very protective. My parents were as well, you see. And my mother-in-law was a widow from the First World

War and when we moved into our house in Portsmouth she came to live with us and I had her living with me for over twenty years. She was very precise and what she said went and through being isolated, I suppose, and because I'd been taught to always respect older people, I did everything I was told. She died only about four years before my husband was taken ill, so I hadn't much freedom all the time I was in England. Sometimes my husband was away for up to two years so I had to keep an eye on my parents and look after my mother-in-law and my two children . . . When my husband died and my mother-in-law and my parents were also dead and my children had left home, I was suddenly faced with a completely different sort of life. Looking back now I don't know what it was that gave me the courage to come out here.

She first came over on the Ten Pound Fare to see her son, who had settled and married in Australia, and she was intending to stay just for the two years to see what it was like. She had only been abroad once – on a holiday to the Rhineland with her husband:

I was a bit apprehensive about the boat trip and all the rest of it but I definitely didn't want to stop in my house on my own. There wasn't anything to keep me there . . . When I arrived here I went to stay with my son and his wife (he'd married a girlfriend from England who came over here when he had set himself up), but I didn't want to be dependent on them so I decided to get a job. I took a job selling encyclopaedias and that meant I was able to travel around and see different places. There was a team of

five of us and we all went round together in the
same car . . . We didn't get any sort of basic salary –
we paid our own way and hoped to get it back on
the commissions. We never stayed in very grand
hotels but they were quite nice. We usually got
enough orders to cover our costs. I really took the
job because I enjoyed travelling – we went to all
sorts of different places around Perth. We went to
some quite remote places like Kalgoorlie, out in the
bush, and usually the people there were keen to
have a chat even if they didn't want to buy an encyclo-
paedia . . .

Really when I moved here it was like moving into
a different world. Before I came out I never really
felt I could cope with the outside world – I'd been so
shielded by my husband, my mother-in-law and my
parents. It was very exciting to find that I could
cope and could travel to all sorts of places on my
own. Since I've been here I've become a different
person.

4

SETTLING IN

For those who could adapt to the Australian way of life, there were many advantages: better job opportunities, a healthier, more informal life-style (particularly in the 1950s) and usually, after a few years, a higher standard of living. One man who settled in the Fifties and has established a successful media and marketing business said:

I enjoyed the sense of enterprise in Australia. If you wanted to do something over here and you had the intelligence and ability to do it, there was nothing to stop you. It gave you the opportunity to try out new things. In England you felt more confined. That's the way I felt about it when I first came out here. I don't know if it's the same now. Migrants who have come over here with nothing have been able to create business empires which they would never have done in their own country because the traditional shackles would have held them back. Really, being able to see possible opportunities for advancement is a state of mind. Coming to a new country you are more geared up to looking for opportunities. Now, if I went back to England and started to get myself set up over there, I would probably find lots of opportunities there because my mental attitudes are different and I'd have the confidence to do things I wouldn't have thought of doing before I came to Australia. When I go back to

England on visits I notice the sort of procrastination that takes place all the time. Often when I'm there on business I find I accomplish in three days of meetings and what-have-you about the same as I'd accomplish in half a day over here. I often feel like a brazen Aussie in my own country.

In the Fifties in Australia, conditions in the factories and conditions of work generally were usually more primitive than they were in Britain and many British workers resented the treatment they received in the work place. It was often the poor working conditions and, particularly in potentially dangerous jobs, the lack of safety precautions at work that led to British workers becoming involved in setting up trades unions. One nineteen year old who went over to Perth as an apprentice moulder said:

I was told I'd be able to continue my apprenticeship out here but there wasn't the same kind of system as you get in England. The employment officer sent Dad and I up to Tomlinsons in Welshpool – we walked all the way up there – because they were looking for a tool machinist and when we got up there – the Employment Officer had explained that I'd done three years' apprenticeship as a moulder in England and was wanting to continue over here so they said I should come up too – we found that they didn't have specialist trades. In England you're either a horizontal borer, a vertical borer, a slotter, a horizontal machinist, a vertical machinist, whereas here you're just a bloody handyman, you had to be a jack of all trades and they were working on obsolete machinery to what we were used to in the UK. If you're a tool machinist in the UK you're used to working to very fine tolerances but the machinery Dad was supposed to work on meant you couldn't work to those tolerances because the machinery just wasn't modern enough. He was also expected to tidy up, sweep the floor and what-have-you and he said, 'What you want is a bloody odd job man here, not a tradesman. I'm a tradesman, I don't do labouring work, it's as simple as that.' In England, there were the tradesmen who just did their particular trade and the labourers who did all the sweeping up.

He also found that some of his work colleagues resented the British Pom but, once he got to know them better, he became accepted and made friends:

There was a certain amount of hostility at work towards Poms. They'd say things like 'The only good Pom is a bloody dead Pom', that sort of thing, but it wasn't too serious. A couple of guys on the spray team used to call me a 'Pommy pig' but I just shrugged it off, ignored it. I didn't find out till later that the word 'bastard' was a term of endearment and that when you were called 'Pommy B' or 'Pommy Bastard' it meant that you'd been accepted. In England it wasn't a term you ever used, it was considered dreadful to call someone a bastard. Also Australians would quite happily call a woman a 'cow' – 'Get out of here, you old cow' and that sort of thing and it didn't mean anything particularly rude, whereas 'cow' in England meant a prostitute. It took me a long time to work out how the Australian mind works. For instance, 'bloody Pom' or 'bloody Pommy' is an insult but 'Pommy bastard' is OK. I took umbrage the first time I was called a 'Pommy B'. It had to be carefully explained to me that in fact that meant I was accepted.

I must admit I suppose I was a typical Pom when I first came out here. I used to say 'We did things this way in England' and they'd say 'You're in Australia now.' I realized that they didn't want to know what we did in the UK, they were quite content doing it their way so I thought 'OK, let them carry on' and I did it my way and let them do it their way.

He later decided to leave the foundry because the conditions were so bad:

I saw men of forty in the foundry looking more like sixty years of age, what with breathing in smoke and fumes, it was so hot and dirty, and I thought to myself 'I'm going to be an old man before I'm a young man', so I got out and found a job in the hospital where I've been working ever since. I saw an advertisement in the paper and I applied and got started as a warden assistant. I've been there twenty years now and I'm working in the physiotherapy department. I'm not a qualified physiotherapist but after eight years working in physio I know as much as what the physiotherapist does. My boss – although she shouldn't do it – always asks me for advice on what she should do because I've had a lot more experience in working with patients than what she has and she usually takes my advice. People respect you more if you've had a lot of work experience over here. They're less worried about bits of paper.

He now has a large and comfortable house in a

pleasant suburb of Perth and feels that his life-style and standard of living is much better than it would have been in England. He enjoys the good weather, the outdoor life and more informal way of doing things – suddenly taking off for an expedition at the weekend with his wife and their caravan or going down to the nearby beach after work for a swim.

Looking back now, I'm very glad my parents decided to come out to Australia. I've had a much better life out here than I would have had in England and I never miss the place now and I've no interest in going back there. It's strange to think that Dad, who was so keen to come out here, is now the one who is homesick for England and the rest of the family have completely settled down here.

Although most British Poms who stayed and settled in the Fifties often enjoyed a higher standard of living in Australia than they had had in the UK, there were some who felt that they could have been better off if they had not emigrated. One Scottish couple who went to Australia when the husband was thirty-nine and the wife thirty-five, decided to emigrate because they did not think they would be able to buy a larger farm in Scotland for a price that they could afford. The husband said:

I was dairy farming and what I'd really wanted was a farm with a cottage on it so that when my son was old enough he would have moved into the cottage and gradually taken over the management of the farm and I'd have stayed on as a sort of adviser. I was hoping to buy a larger farm but I couldn't find anything within my means. I'd scanned all the local papers for farms and I gave up hope of finding what I was looking for at a price I could afford, so I decided to come to Australia. Strangely enough, just after we'd definitely decided to come out here, the bank manager offered me another farm with 160 acres at ten thousand pounds which I could have afforded.

They still think rather wistfully about the farm in Scotland which could now be worth a great deal but as his wife explained:

> The bank manager asked us to have second thoughts but my husband said to me, 'Well, if we don't go to Australia now, you'll always think you've missed something.' So that's why we're here.

They went to Perth and the husband got a job as a farmhand on a big farm in a remote part of the country:

> . . . I got a job on a farm way out in the country in Ballidu. We were given a house to go with the job. It wasn't in a very good state when we arrived but I told them that if they got the paint, I would paint it, so that's what we did. We were able to keep our own hens and a cow there. Of course, it wasn't the same as running your own farm but I realized I'd have to take what jobs I could when I first got here. It was a very big farm – 75,000 acres – and they had a lot of up-to-date machinery but they were behind in their farming methods. I was driving the tractors, being a farm worker. It was in a very remote spot, fourteen miles from the nearest school. We did have

one neighbour about half a mile away, we were lucky. He was a farmer, another Scotsman, and we had another neighbour who worked on the same farm as me and he was six miles away.

Although he did not regret the loss of his farm as much as the rest of the family because it had been a seven-days-a-week job and had caused him a lot of financial worries, his wife and daughter hated being uprooted and felt isolated and lonely in the Australian outback. His wife had liked living on the farm in Scotland. Although she and the family had had to work hard to help keep the farm going, she enjoyed the fact that the whole family was involved and that neighbours called in regularly and the nearest town was only a short bus journey away:

Actually we were in a good wee spot in Scotland because we were only three miles from town and I could get a bus every hour into town if I wanted. I didn't even have to drive the car. We were very happy there. Our children loved it.

It was a big wrench for us to leave and particularly for our eldest daughter. She was fourteen and the education in Australia was way behind the standard in Scotland. To continue her education over here we would have had to send her down to Perth and pay for her board and lodging which we couldn't afford at that time, so she had to leave off her education then and start work. You could leave school at fourteen in Australia if you had a job to go to. She worked with me for a while at a service station but when she was about sixteen we sent her to a business college when we were living in Perth.

The wife could not stand the isolation of living on the farm in Ballidu so they returned to Perth and bought a house there with their savings:

We sold our farm in Scotland quite well and when we left the farm in Ballidu and came back to Perth we bought our house with the money we got for it, so it helped to set us up over here. I started working for Chamberlains, then, the tractor people. I was lucky to get a job as I was then over forty and they thought you were past it when you were over thirty in those days. Jobs were hard to come by.

They both missed the community life they had enjoyed in Scotland:

One of the main differences between here and Scotland is that over there you were automatically part of a community. The minister would come and call on you, you'd be expected to take part in local events. Here you have to create a social life for yourself. In Scotland the community was very close-knit and if you hadn't seen a person for a while you'd go to their house and find out if there was anything wrong with them and make sure they were keeping well. In that way it is much harder over here and life is very cheap. There's no neighbourliness in that sense.

I remember going down a road one day in the country and seeing a sheep that had got out and was dying for lack of water. When I passed that way again some time later it was still out. In Scotland if someone saw a sheep out they'd return it to the others but over here a farmer might easily resent it. You're meant to mind your own business.

Nobody trusts anybody here. It's not safe to do so. In Scotland if you did a deal with someone you could be sure they'd honour it, whereas here you'd never do that, you wouldn't just make a verbal agreement about something in that way.

Although they both think that their values and attitudes have remained unchanged, they have gradually adapted to the Australian way of life but they found it hard to give up their old habits and customs:

It took us five or six years before we gave up having our traditional Christmas dinner. My wife would be getting the kids to eat hot Christmas pudding when the temperature was in the eighties but it just seemed stupid after a while, so we gave up in the end.

Although they are now settled in Australia and would never leave because they have their children and grandchildren living near them, they still go back to Scotland for their holidays and the walls of their house are covered with views of their Scottish farm. If the offer of the nearby, larger farm had been made to them a few months earlier, they both agree that they would never have left Scotland.

The Scottish couple were quite unusual in their pattern of work because they went from being self-employed to becoming employees. Many British Poms found that Australia provided them with an opportunity they had never had — or had never considered in Britain — of starting up their own business. One married woman, who had worked in a hairdressing salon in the UK, met up with another British hair-

dresser in Melbourne who suggested that she should
start up her own salon:

> One day she came over to see me and said to me,
> 'Why don't you start up a business of your own?' I
> laughed and said, 'Oh, I don't know, I've never
> thought about it.' She said, 'Well, I'm going to send
> a man from the Master Ladies' Hairdressing Associa-
> tion to see you.' And the next day he did come and
> one thing led to another. We'd already put down a
> deposit on a house and this gentleman said, 'I've got
> a lovely little salon for you. Would you like to come
> and see it?' So I said, 'Well, I don't know.' He said,
> 'You're very silly if you don't take it because it's a
> beautiful area. It's a place called Camberwell, there's
> a beautiful school for your children to go to and
> you've got living quarters.' So anyhow our ears
> pricked up a bit and we went round and right there
> and then we said we'd take it and I had to move in
> almost immediately. The business was very run
> down but after I did two or three ladies they passed
> me on to someone else. One customer would recom-
> mend me to another so in time I was able to take on
> an apprentice and after that I took a fully qualified
> girl. In the end I had a staff of four and it was quite a
> big salon. After two years we raised a mortgage to
> buy the salon.

She found that running the salon changed her personality as well as giving her financial independence:

> Australia has been very kind to us, very good. I
> think it changed us all quite a bit. In England I
> always did whatever my husband wanted to do, but

once I got the salon over here I wasn't going to be pushed around by anybody. By making a life for myself over here, I got a lot of confidence in myself. Now I belong to a number of different clubs and I find I can get up and speak to an audience which I could never have done in England. Having a strong-minded husband and a strong-minded mother, I was used to going along with what other people wanted me to do, but now I can stand up for myself.

Sadly, not all the British Poms' enterprises turned out so successfully. Some thought that fortunes would fall in their laps quite effortlessly. The ones who suc-ceeded usually worked long hours and put a lot of effort into their businesses to get them off the ground. One young couple who went to Sydney, where the husband started up a printing business, found that the business finally drove them apart although the wife, who was hardworking and took on the responsibility for running most of her husband's business as well as doing a full-time job herself, was unable to save the whole venture. When they first arrived in Sydney they both took full-time jobs. Everything was going quite well until five or six years later when they had had their first child and had saved up enough for a deposit to buy a shop:

It was then my husband started up his own little printing business and there was quite a demand for printing wedding stationery and that kind of thing. If he'd been a properly qualified printer he might have done quite well but he couldn't do the printing himself, so we had to hire a printer. He started off in a partnership but the other man got cheesed off because he found he was doing all the work. My husband then set up another partnership and the same thing happened. I was quite enthusiastic when the business started off but as things went on and I kept coming home from my job to find my husband reading the paper, never working, I became more and more disillusioned. There was always work stacked up waiting to be done but my husband couldn't have organized a Teddy Bears' Picnic. He wasn't even capable of delivering an invoice to the building next to him. It would have been for around six thousand dollars and it was in his pocket for six weeks. I made a special trip to put it in myself because I knew if I didn't it would never have got delivered. He really was hopeless ... There was always plenty of work; the business was never short of work. It was getting it done in time that was the problem. I used to come home from working at my job all day and do the books for him and the typing. All my daylight hours I was working, often typing till midnight. I would get up at five in the morning to finish off jobs for the business before I left for work. I couldn't get my husband out of bed. We lived in a flat above the shop but at nine o'clock in the morning he would still be in bed when the printer arrived. The printer would often be waiting for half an hour doing nothing because he was still in bed. We had constant rows about this and there were two occasions when I got a bit of a thumping-up — he wasn't violent as a matter of course — and I spent a lot of time crying at that stage. We were always getting summonses and things like that. His problem was that he could never face up to reality.

Their marriage ended in divorce and she returned home to England with the children for a while but eventually decided that life as a single parent was better in Australia:

I think I've managed better as a single parent over here than I would have done in England. Salaries were higher over here, for instance, when we split up. Since I've been on my own I've never run into any serious financial problems although it was all a bit of a struggle to begin with. I am the General Manager's secretary; I get the highest secretarial wage in the company but secretaries over here aren't paid a great deal. Fortunately I happen to be pretty handy about the house. I put the doors on myself, fix the roof if the tiles are broken. I'm an expert at finding a bargain and making money go a long way! I can make my own clothes.

I find that I no longer socialize with married couples any more because once you're a single parent you're different but I have joined an organization called 'Parents without Partners' which has a bit of a reputation for being a pick-up place – which it can be if you want it to be – but I've found it tremendous because it means there's always somewhere to go dancing and I love dancing. As far as the opposite sex is concerned they've been a bit of a dead loss but I can go out any night of the week to some function and I've met quite a few very nice ladies through it who are good friends now. I've certainly had a better time in the last ten years alone than I ever had when I was married. Being with my husband was one long worry and hassle.

Some couples found that the challenge of coping with a new environment brought them much closer together but marriages that were not particularly satisfactory to begin with often collapsed when the couple reached Australia. Many found that, having changed their life-style, they were less prepared to put up with an unsatisfactory relationship. One unhappily married man, who came to Australia hoping that new circumstances might improve his marriage, found that the situation only got worse and he eventually solved the problem by packing his wife home to England:

I had a lot of personal problems when I first came to Australia because my wife didn't like it over here. She was a lot older than me. She was twenty-three when we got married and I was sixteen. My mother died when I was very small. We were looked after by my father. I was the youngest and the only one left at home and my father was getting old. I suppose I was looking for a mother figure but my wife was anything but motherly. She was a hot-tempered Welsh girl and I got the opposite. Eventually she went back to England and by the time I got the divorce we'd been officially married fifteen years. When she went home I was already involved with the girl I finally married. She was my secretary. She'd been married to a Scotchman who was knocking her around so she wasn't very happy. She was ten years my junior. My wife had been saying all the time that she wanted to go back to England. When she flew into a temper she became violent. If she couldn't get her own way she would fall down in a faint wherever she was. I put up with her for a long time but in the end she went on about England so much that I gave her her fare and let her take one of our two sons along with her and put her on the boat back.

Once his wife had left and he had settled down with his new girlfriend, who was an Australian, his business career began to take off; he started another family and later adopted a part-aboriginal child:

I was always ambitious and when I met Fay, the secretary who became my girlfriend, we got together our own furnishing company and we were doing about a million dollars a year. Then I developed another company from there and I had one in Singapore too. I used to fly over to the UK about once a year and go down to Singapore and South-East Asia about once a month. I was still technically married at this time but Fay and I were living together and she changed her name by deed poll. We had two children, a son and a daughter, then we were going to have another one and it died in the womb. Of course, Fay got very upset so we decided to adopt another child and we took on a part-aboriginal boy who was the same age as the child we would have had and it's worked out beautifully. He's nearly fifteen now, a lovely boy. He's half Australian, half aboriginal, quite a handsome-looking lad. He was only a few weeks old when we got him. I took my other two kids with me and we went to his foster mother's house and my two kids loved him. There was only one problem, the welfare lass came round and she said, 'I'm sorry, we've never had this before, your background is perfect, your income, your home, your life-style, your other two kids, but how can you adopt if you're not married?' I suppose I was still wary of marriage but after that we decided to get married. This time it has been absolutely fantastic. Very seldom, about once a year, we have a shouting match, but that's all. I suppose we got together in the first place just to have an affair because we were both having such a bad time with our marriages but as time wore on I realized this was the one.

They had no problems bringing up their aboriginal child, perhaps because from the start they never thought of him as being different:

> Our aboriginal child fitted in quite naturally with the rest of us; we never thought of him as any different. I've never taken any particular interest in the aborigines; so far as I was concerned he was just one of us. He never seemed interested in his real parents and they never got in touch with him. He's one of those kids who's never been a problem. He does everything right. He doesn't talk very much but we're very fond of each other.

After making a success in business in Australia, the whole family returned to England for a while (he was by then divorced from his first wife, who had remarried). They had hoped to buy and run a country pub but things did not work out as they had expected:

> When I'd sold one of the businesses well, I thought it might be nice to go back and run a country pub in England, but we had a lot of hassle trying to buy the business and decided to come back to Australia. I first went back to England in '69 be-

cause I wanted the family to know how well I'd done. We were the roughest kids in the street. My father would cut up an old overcoat to make trousers for us and we never had any underpants. If our boots were being repaired we had to stay in until they were ready. We were bloody poor. I've made enough money now not to have to work again but I still do work because, when I took some time off, I got bored to tears. I thought I'd like playing golf every day; I love playing golf. But I lost interest in it when it was no longer a special treat. It was the same with fishing. It was OK doing these things when I had to make the time to do so. I'm now running the public relations and sales side of one of the big laboratories in Perth. I saw an ad in the paper for the job and applied and got it. I had to sell my companies because I was offered such a lot for them but I'm very glad to be back at work again.

Another couple, who were not particularly unhappy with each other, also separated because the wife felt homesick for England and eventually returned to live there:

Whilst I grew to like Australia more and more, my wife grew to hate it. Over the years she began to loathe living in Australia and she hated the thought of our daughters growing up and marrying and settling down over here. I'm not sure exactly what she disliked about Australia but I think it may have been the Australian man's way of life. Australian men spend a lot of time with each other; they often go on drinking binges in the evenings and fishing trips at week-ends, leaving the wife and family at home. A lot

of Australian wives accept this as quite natural and
we had a lot of neighbours who lived like this and it
may not have been the kind of life my wife wanted
for her daughters. She eventually went back to England and we separated about ten years ago.

Before they finally separated, the whole family went
back to England for about a year and the wife hoped
her husband would want to stay while he hoped she
would want to return to Australia:

> We'd leased a shop we owned in Sydney so what
> with that and the income from savings we could live
> quite comfortably in the UK for a while . . . But I
> needed to earn a living and it was quite obvious I
> couldn't earn a living and keep us in the life-style we
> were used to in England. It's never been difficult for
> me to find employment in Australia. My wife refused
> to return with me and she stayed on in accommoda-
> tion we'd rented in England. The boys stayed with
> her and went to public school in England. I didn't
> mind about this because I suspected that the boys
> would want to return to Australia eventually. I
> couldn't see anything that would keep them over
> there. Now two of them have returned here and
> there's just one in the UK. My two daughters are in
> England as well . . .
> We'd been married for twenty years before we
> split up and we hadn't had a bad marriage in many
> ways, but my wife was very close to her mother and
> that may have been one of the main reasons why she
> wanted to be in England. She never made any friends
> in Australia although she belonged to a tennis club
> but she often preferred reading on her own to going

out. It is true she had five young children then so she didn't have all that much spare time and we didn't go out to parties very often. When I set up my own business in Australia we were both very involved with that, working very hard, so in the last five years of our life in Australia we were both extremely busy. People don't call in much over here in the informal way they do in England where neighbours and friends pop in for a cup of tea. My wife missed the support of close friends and relatives.

Although some of the children later followed him back to Australia, he returned there alone:

When I came back to Australia I really had to start all over again financially. Our old house and its contents were sold to support my ex-wife and provide for the children and their education. It was easier building up the second time than the first because I was on my own. I didn't feel too upset about this. I just accepted that I was no longer a married man with five children but an ex-married man with children who had flown the coop. I didn't have any great feelings of remorse although I was disappointed it had happened.

He gradually built up a new life for himself and three years after his return he remarried:

When I first came back to Sydney I went to live with a nephew for a few weeks and then I rented a house. I lived there for about six months on my own but I decided after that to share a flat with another fellow because I found it lonely living on my own. I was being employed by a company as a consultant and I was also involved in merchandizing. Just about the end of my time with that company I met Anne, who is now my new wife.

Anne and I met at a dance function at a nearby bowling club. Anne was with her parents and I was with a friend on that particular evening. We were sitting at the same table and we got talking, danced. Later on I had an open-day party at the flat where I was living and Anne came along as one of the guests. The following evening we went out to dinner together and from then on we were friends. Six months later we were husband and wife!

Perhaps partly because the Ten Pound Poms were by nature enterprising and because they had already got used to uprooting and starting a new life elsewhere, they seemed to be good at rebuilding their lives and adapting to changing circumstances. Their attitudes to dramas and crises were often more relaxed than those of many English families who would have been more susceptible to social conventions and fears of what the neighbours would say. Many immigrants found a sense of freedom in Australia because they could escape from the conventions of their social class, which were far more rigid in the England of the Fifties, family obligations and a tight-knit gossipy community. In Australia they found that friendships could be established without too many questions being asked, people would accept you for what you were. In work too, your experience and whether or not you could do the job was more important than whether you had all the necessary qualifications. This gave many immigrants the opportunity to build up careers in new fields and take up a variety of jobs instead of sticking to one particular trade or line of business.

Sometimes the opportunities available to those who were not properly qualified for the job were almost too good. One man who had spent three years in the British Army and had returned to England after being stationed in Malaya found that he could not get a job near his home town because they did not like ex-army people. He decided to emigrate and on the day he arrived in Perth he was offered a job as a surveyor's off-sider. After gaining some experience working on some big projects, he found he was being offered jobs that should have been undertaken by fully-qualified surveyors:

> I think I was stretching myself a lot in those days. Most of the jobs I was doing I wasn't properly qualified for. I got them because I had a good track record and I had the experience but I was always swimming a bit out of my depth . . . I worked on some very big surveying projects, including the Sydney Opera House – I was on that for six months working on the roof. But as time went on a lot of younger, well-qualified surveyors were coming into the game and the competition was getting tougher. I had to rely on the contacts I'd made, people who knew what I'd done, but I was always having to push into new fields that I didn't know that much about – I've worked on drainage, bridges, tunnels – I was continually learning new skills very quickly and I had to be responsible for these big projects. Often the younger men under me were far better qualified and the only way I could keep on top of them was by having more work experience. When calculators

came along, for instance, these younger people could use them and work twice as fast as I could, whereas I'd never used a calculator before. The only way I could beat them was by having a particular kind of cunning based on a life's experience in the trade. These younger blokes, for instance, could work out the cost of a particular building far quicker than me, but I'd know about short cuts that would work. When computers came along I didn't know a thing about them so I had to go to school to learn that, which I did. I learnt just enough to handle them in my work. All my learning was just to get by, I didn't have time for more.

The work eventually proved too much for him, and when he was thirty-five he suffered from high blood pressure. Since then he has also had kidney trouble:

I'm on fairly strong drugs now and have to cope with the side-effects of these. I was told by my doctor that I would have to lead a very quiet life or I'd burst a blood vessel. I was about thirty-five when I became ill; I'm thirty-nine now. I did buy a house but it was just at the time when I became ill and interest rates went soaring up so I wasn't able to take on that kind of financial burden. Wages were being frozen then and, although I didn't stop work, I had to stop doing the highly paid work I had been doing and in the end I had to sell the house for a small loss. It was a big old house and I'd planned to do it all up so I was disappointed when we had to sell it. I now live in a much smaller rented house and I find it far too cramped but the children are growing up and leaving home now.

Because he has suffered badly from the strain of not being properly qualified, he has seen to it that his children have proper professional qualifications but, in spite of his illness and the financial setbacks that this has brought about, he does not regret going to Australia:

> I'm glad I came to Australia for the children's sake and for my own. I feel I've learned a lot over here and had a very varied and interesting life, and my children have a better chance over here to do well for themselves. The only thing, as far as my children are concerned, is that I feel Perth is very cut off from the rest of the world and I would like them to be able to go back and visit England. I'm afraid that they may become rather narrow-minded if they don't travel a bit and I would like them to know about the English way of life ... The one good thing about my illness is that I've seen much more of my children and become much closer to them.

Australia is in some ways a tough society. In spite of their more relaxed attitude, Australians as a whole are not sympathetic to losers, and immigrants who fail do not have the support and back-up of old friends and relations that they would have in their home country. As one Ten Pound Pom said:

> It is a classless society here but money does count. Having the right kind of possessions is important and if you don't own a house by a certain age people begin to think you've failed.

For those who succeed there are enormous advanvantages. The combination of good weather, a beautiful coastline, miles and miles of unspoilt country, and a general attitude that for those who can afford it, any sport or hobby is open to them, means that a wide variety of interests is available to the New Australians. The Poms who made good found that it was not just their working lives which changed dramatically. Many took on new pursuits and developed skills that they would never have acquired if they had stayed in Britain.

5

GOING
HOME

*Q*uite a number of migrants returned to Britain after two years and some went back even before their two years were up. Those who left Australia within the first two years had to pay the balance of their passage out, as well as meet the costs of their passage back. Some, who wanted to return, were never able to raise the money to do so. 'There were people who stayed in the hostels for years,' said one returnee. 'They just couldn't get their act together and they'd spend time moaning about the conditions, whereas others would get jobs and be out of the hostel within a few days.'

Those who went back to Britain left for a variety of reasons; by no means all of them were dissatisfied with life in Australia. Some went for family reasons, others because of financial considerations and quite a number returned after two years because they had gone over on a working holiday and had never intended to stay. When the Australian Government raised its target for immigrants, the greater numbers required meant that a wider range of people were accepted and some might not have been suited to adapting to life in a new country. There was often a high level of departures following a big push for immigrants.

Many young couples left in their twenties when their parents were still fit and well. In some cases, by the time they had reached their thirties and forties, the migrants were faced with the problem of one parent dying, leaving the other alone, or with a sick relation who needed care and attention. Sometimes family members in Britain took over these responsibilities, but some found that they had to return home and many left Australia intending to come back in a few months' or a few years' time. Once they had gone home and settled back into their old way of life, they often found it difficult to leave again. One returnee, who had always regretted leaving Australia, said:

> I came back because my father had died and my mother wasn't very well and then I met up with a girl I later married. She was very attached to her mother, so we ended up staying on in England. It wasn't what I had planned at all; I didn't even bother to unpack when I first arrived. I thought I'd be on a boat back to Australia within a few weeks.

Another girl who had gone out initially on a working holiday, and had enjoyed it so much she intended to stay, also found herself returning home reluctantly when her father died and her mother could not cope on her own.

> If it hadn't been for my mother I would have been very happy to stay in Australia. I went out there when I was twenty-six and the boat journey was the best holiday I've ever had. I went to Sydney where I stayed in a hostel I didn't much like but I got myself a job nine hours after my arrival, so I was able to move out and share lodgings in Sydney with some friends of my sister. I took temporary jobs so that I could move on and travel all over Australia. After the first four months I decided to try for a job as a

cook on a sheep station so that I could see some of the outback but they needed someone who could make bread and that was outside my range of skills. I didn't realize, till friends told me later, that bread wasn't all that difficult to make. Instead I got a job as a general hand on a sheep station north west of Brisbane where I lived in a nice house with the farmer and his wife and spent most of my time in the shearing sheds picking up the fleece. I was well looked after but I was very shocked by their treatment of the aborigines. They were treated almost like slaves and had to live in these corrugated iron shacks. There was total segregation. They were never allowed to eat with us and the conditions they lived in were worse than the animals'. I left Brisbane after four months because I'd been invited by a friend I made on board ship to go to her wedding in Adelaide. Then I got a job as a waitress in the Snowy Mountains, one of the most popular holiday resorts. It was rather a grand restaurant but I got some tips from a New Zealand girl who worked there on silver service waitressing – how to cope with the different wines and all that. Because I was a Pom, the manager picked me out to be a nanny to his children so I moved out of the staff lodge and into the manager's home. The family ate every night at the restaurant and I ate with them, so I found myself being waited on by all my former colleagues. The other waitresses resented me a bit for this. They knew that I'd been given the job because I was a Pom and the manager thought it would be smart to have an English nanny. I had a wonderful time with him and his family. They used to take me out on their yacht at weekends and I didn't really have to do very much but I didn't want to stay too long. My plan was to keep moving on.

The longest job I did was with a car company in Sydney working in the sales department which I did for six months. While I was there a chap in his fifties turned up to buy a car and when he heard my accent he said, 'Oh, you're one of our Ten Pound Poms are you? Would you like to come and spend the weekend with my wife and me?' It wasn't the sort of thing I'd ever have done with a stranger in England but in Australia it seemed perfectly all right and I had a wonderful weekend with them and still keep in touch. When my younger sister went to Australia they were very hospitable to her. In England you are more inhibited by all the different class distinctions. I now work in the Civil Service where you are made very aware of your place and who are your superiors but in Australia it was so free and easy. People seem genuinely friendly and keen to know you, regardless of the kind of job you're doing. Now I'm back in England and sharing a maisonette with my mother, who needs looking after. I found it quite easy to settle in when I came home but I look back on the two years I spent in Australia as some of the best times I've ever had. It was marvellous to be completely free and to be able to do exactly what I liked. One day I wouldn't mind going back to live in Australia again and settle there.

Quite a number of returnees never completely break their ties with Australia and some have gone back and forth between the two countries a number of times. One man who went out on the Big Brother Movement in 19151 when he was seventeen has gone back to

Australia several times since his first visit and is still considering settling there.

The Big Brother Movement was a junior immigration scheme for boys between the ages of sixteen and nineteen. The boys went out for half the price of the normal assisted passage fare, five pounds instead of ten pounds. They were taken out by Big Brothers, adult members of the Movement, who looked after them. Many of the boys were trained to work on the land but some went into industry and other forms of employment. The Movement only operated in New South Wales. The majority of the boys went to a training farm in Liverpool, a suburb of Sydney.

I didn't go there to work on the land. I was on a new scheme set up for some of the B.B.M. boys to work in industry in Sydney. The Little Brothers' jobs were arranged for them by the Movement's employment officer – in my day he was a policeman – and boys were employed in a variety of industries depending on their skills. I worked in an Oxide lending lab in Alexandria, a suburb of Sydney. The managing director of the company was a Big Brother. The Big Brothers were usually well-established men of good character and all the Little Brothers had a Big Brother to help them out when they arrived in Australia. Mine was the chairman and managing director of an insurance company. I was disappointed because he only saw me a couple of times for a grand lunch. Maybe he didn't feel I was a lost little kid. He was meant to be responsible for sorting out any problems I might have settling in. [All the Big Brothers went through a selection process to ascertain whether or not they were suitable to take part in the Scheme.]

When we arrived in Australia we were sent to a special boys' hostel. I was sent to one in a suburb of Sydney. It was a shock after being treated like kings on board ship and having had all those wonderful meals to be back in what seemed like a very regimented orphanage. We were treated like little criminals. We weren't allowed out except at weekends and the food was dreadful. As soon as I'd got a job I moved out of the hostel into a boarding-house, which was approved by the Movement, and which was more homely. The hostel was just meant to be a temporary residence for us while we were settling in and finding our feet. I stayed with a lady who ran a lodging-house in Botany, another suburb of Sydney, and I got involved in the local church. I had left the Oxide lending lab by then and got a job with an airline which only operated in New South Wales. I worked in the office on reservations for a while and then I was called up for National Service. [At that time, all eighteen year olds had to do some form of National Service. Later it operated on a lottery basis and people were selected by their date of birth.]

I was called up for the air force and had to do a six-month active service and three and a half years on the Reserve which meant I had to get permission from the Australian Government if I wanted to leave the country any time during that period. None of us came out with any rank after our six months. I went in as an Aircraftsman Recruit Minor (A.C.R.M.) and I came out as an Aircraftsman (A.C.). My mustering was a clerk administrative assistant which meant I was working in the armoury. I was mostly involved in office procedures dealing with guns which were usually obsolete. They'd been in storage since 1939. I was lucky because it was before Vietnam and after Korea – I was called up in about '53 or '54 – so I didn't get involved in any fighting. We were stationed at Bankstown, another suburb of Sydney, and lived in service huts, about thirty of us to a hut. The work wasn't at all demanding and the food was extremely good but I considered the whole thing to be a complete waste of time. It did help some boys to be disciplined and to learn to become more independent but I was on my own anyway. I got so fed up that I went A.W.O.L. (absent without leave), and I decided to take a train back to Sydney but some of the other National Service trainees, who got wind of what I was doing, drove in to find me at the station and persuaded me to go back. After I'd done Australian National Service, I was determined that I wasn't going to get called up for another bout if I went back to Britain. In those days, if I had remained a British citizen, I could have been called up again if I'd returned to the UK, so I decided to become an Australian citizen. It was quite easy to become an Australian citizen then if you were a British subject. There wasn't any ceremony or anything, you just filled in the necessary forms and were issued with a document of citizenship. Until then all I'd had was a document of identity (which was what we had to have before coming to Australia) and I could have stayed on indefinitely in Australia with this I.D. paper if I hadn't wanted to become an Australian citizen. [He went back to the UK in 1956 because he wanted to spend his twenty-first birthday with his family. He found that he could not settle at his family's home in the country so he went to

London and worked for the Big Brother organization based at Australia House.]

I worked as Assistant Secretary to the Secretary
of the Big Brother Movement, who was a retired
naval commander. I used to go all over the UK
addressing groups of boys about the Movement,
which was non-sectarian, non-political and non-
profit-making. It was also a rule of the Movement
that we shouldn't advertise because it was thought
better if our reputation was spread by word of
mouth. I would talk to boys who had applied for the
Scheme and to their parents and answer any queries
they might have. I also interviewed the boys who
applied. I had to check out whether they had any
criminal records and assess whether they were going
to be able to adapt to the Australian way of life.
Some boys at that age are very immature and not
able to cope with life in another country. The B.B.M.
Scheme was first set up in 1925 to train boys for
work on the farms but by the time I was involved
they were being employed in jobs ranging from
heavy industry to newspapers. I usually conducted
these interviews at employment bureaux in different
parts of the country. Any boy under eighteen had to
have his parents' permission to go. We didn't usually
recruit boys from orphanages or broken homes –
they would go out on other kinds of schemes like
the Fairbridge Society.

The day before they sailed, we organized a party
for all the boys and their parents in the basement of
Australia House. We would show them a film about
Australia and give them all tea and cakes. One of the
officials from the Immigration Department used to
come as well, so worried parents could ask them any

last-minute questions, but the real aim of the party
was to give the boys a good send-off.

[The boys usually went by boat in groups with
several escorting officers, approved adult volunteers
who liked the idea of a free passage to Australia.]
Many of the escorting officers were schoolmasters
or people like that. I went back to Australia as an
escorting officer in 1957 and took the 2000th B.B.M.
boy out with me. When I arrived in Australia, I
worked for a while as a manager of the same hostel
that I had gone to when I first went out. I was really
just helping out because they needed someone to
run the hostel just then. I hope the boys didn't find
it quite as regimented in my day as it had been when
I first went there. After a few months at the hostel I
rejoined Qantas airways – I had been working for
them before I left for the UK. I had intended to
settle permanently in Australia but I returned to
England in 1974 to be best man at my brother's
wedding; by then my mother's health wasn't too
good so I bought a business over here and decided
to settle here for the rest of her lifetime. I'm still
hoping to live in Australia eventually but I don't
know when that will be.

A great many returnees were single people who decided to take advantage of the Assisted Passage Scheme
to have a two-year holiday and see the world. In the
Fifties there were usually more single boys than girls
who went on their own. Most girls either went out in
organized groups or to join a friend or relations or a
boyfriend, but a few of the more adventurous girls
who travelled on the Scheme did not find it difficult to
work their way around Australia. One girl, whose

father had been in government service in Burma and who was used to travel, went to Australia on her own when she was nineteen, without having a single friend or relation there. She was used to being independent of her family. She had been sent on her own to boarding-school in England while her parents were in Burma, where her father was killed by the Japanese.

I'd always wanted to go to Australia because my mother used to talk about it. She'd been as a young girl. She'd travelled a lot and she never really liked living in England. I suppose it was more unusual in the 1950s for a girl in her teens to travel alone than it is nowadays, but I think it would be far more danger-ous to do so now than it was when I went out there.

[She had trained as a secretary and was working for an advertising agency in London when she heard about the Ten Pound Fare and realized that this would provide her with the ideal opportunity of getting to Australia. As she did not know anyone who could nominate her, she went to Australia House to find out if there was any other way she could go on her own.] I went to Australia House to inquire how I could get out there and there was a very nice man there who said, 'One way you can do it, as you are a shorthand typist, is go and work in Canberra. We can get you out there pretty quickly like that. As a matter of fact, we would get you there next month, or at the end of this month, in a few weeks, if you are ready.' So I said, 'Oh, yes, I'm ready, I can go whenever you like.' He told me that I had to sign some forms and get them back to him by the end of the week. Well, I got up late on Satur-day morning and the office was shut and that was my deadline. He told me that I had to get them to him by then or he wouldn't be able to book me a berth on the next ship going out, the *Stratheden*. When I reached Australia House I found all the doors were locked so I went round the building and found a fire escape. I went up it and, as I knew which floor his office was on, I got in through the fire door and went to his office and knocked on the door. He said, 'Come in,' and when he saw me he was absolutely staggered. He said, 'How on earth did you manage to get in? The building is locked.' When I told him about the fire escape he said, 'Good. That's the sort of person we want in Australia.' I gave him the forms and he managed to get me a berth.

I went to work in the External Territories Department at Canberra because this was the Government department which dealt with New Guinea and I thought I might be able to get to New Guinea that way. In fact the job was so boring and Canberra was one of the dullest places to visit – it's full of Government offices – that I left after a few months and decided to work my way round Australia instead. I'd also been told that New Guinea was full of spiders and snakes and the most horrible things which rather put me off. I thought I would see Australia first. While I was in Canberra I stayed at a Government hostel and I had a little bedroom in this prefab. It was full of foreigners; there were people there from all over the world. The men lived in one section and the women in another and we all went to a big mess building for our meals. There was also an amusement building for table tennis, dancing and all the rest of it.

[She found it quite easy to get along with the

Australians and never came across any serious anti-Pom feelings but she was constantly teased.] They teased me about the dirty English and how they'd never met a clean English person until they met me. They'd say, 'We can't understand it, Laura, you have two or three showers a day, we've never met an English person like you. Your lot only bath once a week, don't you, and you keep coals in the bath.' You see when we were young, if you wanted to insult an English person you said, 'Oh, you're dirty.' In England you might have a bath but you wouldn't bathe in it, you'd keep your coal in it for your fire. It was a well-known joke. So they used to trot that one out on me. They also used to tease me about sport and how we could never win anything in those days. Every time a British football, cricket or rugby team came out, they were absolutely sloshed; we were mercilessly beaten by the Australians. I hate sport but I used to feel it very much. I'd wish to heaven we could win something. I could feel really humiliated by it all. I didn't like the way the Australians made fun of the British but now I'm over here I equally don't like the Australians being denigrated.

[She left Canberra and went to Sydney and Hobart, where she found it quite easy to get temporary work, and then she went to Brisbane.] In Brisbane I got a job with the Imperial Meat Factory; it sounds terrible. I wasn't going to take the job but the salary was good. I went to see the office supervisor and I was going to tell him that I didn't like the idea of working in a meat factory but when I saw the boss I changed my mind. He was just like Ray Milland, the heart-throb actor of our day, and I took the job immediately. He was English and very nice and

kind. I never went out with him because he was
married but we got on well. He had a lot of cattle-
and sheep-buyers coming in because of the meat
trade and, as he knew I wanted to see the outback,
he made arrangements for me to take a job as a
governess in a sheep station in Queensland. In those
days children who were too far away from anywhere
to go to school, had to learn through a correspondence course; now it's all done through TV and
radio. There was a special college which sent out a
whole series of 'lessons' on different subjects and I'd
work through these with the children and then send
their homework back to the college to be corrected.

We were miles from anywhere with no neighbours, and the sheep were all rounded up by the
men on horseback. The family consisted of the husband and wife and their three sons, whom I taught,
and there were several farmhands. The only other
female beside the wife and me was the cook. The
family was very kind to me and said that I could ride
whenever I wanted but that I should be careful about
getting lost. I thought this was daft at first but,
when I went out for a ride, I saw what they meant.
There was scrub for miles and miles and every tree
looks the same. My mother had said to me earlier,
'Don't ask for a saddle in the outback, it looks really
wet and English. If you don't get a saddle, just get
on and get used to it.' When they said, 'All right,
Laura, you can get up on this horse; you don't need
a saddle, do you?' I was terrified but I said, 'No,' as
firmly as I could. It turned out they were just trying
me out and they gave me a saddle after all.

The wife was a lot older than me, in her mid-
thirties, and I preferred her husband, who was a

more straightforward sort of person. She'd been a society woman in Sydney and had had a very different sort of life. She never seemed really settled and lots of the time her mind seemed to be miles away, probably thinking about her friends in Sydney. Her husband adored her and gave her everything she wanted but I think she would have been much happier with a more superficial and glittering life-style.

[After a few months in the outback she decided to go and see the Barrier Reef, where she was offered a job as a waitress. She had heard about the job through her landlady in Brisbane, where she had worked at the meat factory.] While I was in Brisbane, I stayed in this wonderful guest house where the landlady was like a mother to me. One woman I met there had been on Heron Island in the Barrier Reef and she said how wonderful it was. I'd said that I would love to have gone there but I couldn't afford a holiday because it was quite expensive. She told me that I could get a job as a temporary waitress there during the Christmas season. She gave me the name of the big hotel there and I wrote to them. They wrote back saying they would pay my fare over, plus so much a week and free board. I had to take a sea plane which landed in the water and then a little boat came to fetch us to take us to the island. On the sea plane I made friends with some holiday-makers who thought that I was going to be a fellow guest at the hotel. They didn't realize I was going out there to be a waitress. I wanted to tell them before I got there but Australians talk such a lot that it's hard to get a word in sometimes and I was quite shy. When I got to the hotel I was dreading the moment when they would realize that I wasn't one

GOING HOME

of them, I was one of the staff. I was told that I had
to wait at table for the evening meal and when I got
to their table I thought it was going to be very
embarrassing but they took it quite naturally and
were as friendly as ever.

[She never felt worried about running out of
money or having no one to turn to. If problems
arose, she could always go to the nearest branch of
the Bank of New South Wales. It was one of the
largest banks and had branches all over the country.]
My anchor in Australia was the Bank of NSW.
When I first arrived in Sydney, I went in there about
my account and they were so nice to me. All the
people behind the counter were very friendly and
asked me to their homes. They had a wonderful
amateur dramatics society and they used to put on
shows which they invited me to go along to. They
were really like a family to me and I knew, wherever I
went, I could always call in to the nearest branch if
there was any sort of problem and they would help
me out. Everybody knew each other in those days
and one group of people would pass me on to the
next so I never felt worried about going to a new
place. The lodging-houses in those days were very
respectable. I made a lot of friends and had a very
good time but I never formed any deep relationships.
I was always too busy working out where I wanted
to go next and moving on.

[She did keep up a steady correspondence with
the man who was later to become her husband but
she had no thoughts of marriage at that time, she
wanted to see the world first. After travelling round
Australia, she hoped to go on similar trips to other
English-speaking countries – Canada, Rhodesia or

South Africa. On returning to England, after spending nearly three years in Australia, she met up with
her correspondent whom she had first met before
setting out on her travels. After a year's courtship
she reluctantly abandoned her plans for seeing the
rest of the world and agreed to get married.] Nothing
in my life, since my trip to Australia, has ever seemed
quite as exciting. It was partly being young, and on
my own, and seeing so many new things for the first
time. I loved Australia and the Australians and I
would happily go back and live there now but my
husband likes living in England and being near the
rest of his family. My daughter, who is now in her
twenties, is very keen to get to Australia – probably
because, like me with my mother, she has heard so
much about it.

One man who went out when he was seventeen and
a half found that after the six-week voyage, 'which
seemed like one long party', he had to face up to some
harsher realities on arrival in Melbourne.

I didn't take much money out with me but what I
had I spent on the voyage over. When I reached
Melbourne I only had one and sixpence. I'd expected
that I was going to be looked after on arrival in
much the same way as they'd done on board ship.
Before we disembarked they gave me the address of
a hostel that I could go to. It turned out to be a
rather nice-looking lodging-house in quite a good
part of Melbourne – not like the army camps that
lots of people got sent to – but when I turned up,
after walking there from the harbour, it was about
ten o'clock in the evening. I rang the bell and a big

caretaker guy answered the door and said I was too late and that the hostel closed at nine o'clock. I didn't know what to do; eventually I just put my coat down on the pavement outside the hostel and used my rucksack as a pillow and went to sleep there. I felt very fed up with the hostel after that and decided to look for a lodging house but I didn't have any money. Luckily for me I found a very nice lodging-house where another immigrant, one of my fellow lodgers, lent me enough to cover the first week's rent. The following week, I managed to get a job and pay him back.

I stayed in all sorts of lodging-houses during my time in Australia. In Sydney I had a weird landlady, who was seventy-five and skeleton thin, who spent her time going on strange diets. When I was there she was on a grape diet which she claimed cleaned out her system. She was so thin and tired she could hardly walk but she believed in it all passionately and even took me to some lectures to try to convert me. There were a lot of foreign immigrants in the lodging-houses and they'd all have their own way of doing things, so you felt this constant jostle of different cultures going on around you. In Brisbane, there was this woman who always had lambs' brains for breakfast, not the best thing to come down to at seven o'clock in the morning. In Melbourne there was a Jewish bus conductor from Hackney who came home every evening with some bargain that he'd bought which he would try to off-load on to me. On the whole, the English migrants would stick together and so would the Greeks and the Italians. I tended to avoid the migrant cliques because I wanted to get to know the Australians. A lot of the time I was working in restaurants and bars so it wasn't difficult to make friends. I dated one girl I got to know when I was working as a waiter and she came into the restaurant with some of her friends. Her family were very well off so I would go and spend the week-ends with her on her father's boat. It was quite a jet-set sort of existence.

I'd never intended to stay in Australia. As far as I was concerned, I'm English and England is my home. I didn't even stay the full two years because, after moving around from place to place for about eighteen months – I'd been to Melbourne, Canberra, Sydney and Brisbane – I got fed up with starting up a new life in a new place and thought it would be a relief to get home. I managed to work my passage back as a ship's cleaner. I had to pay some of my fare back because I didn't stay the full two years but it still worked out as a great bargain and I got back home with enough money saved up to buy myself an MG Midget sports car.

It may have been partly because I was young and impressionable at that time but Australia has been one of the most vivid experiences of my life. I also think it made me a more tolerant and a more amenable sort of person. I'd been head boy of my school and I'd always done quite well at everything and I was quite pleased with myself. It was good for me to come up against a whole lot of different kinds of people and have to survive as a Pommy migrant. The Australians preferred almost any other kind of migrant to a Pom but they're good at accepting you for what you are, if you learn to get along with them.

Not all the young singles went just for a holiday;

some seriously intended to stay in Australia and make a life for themselves out there if everything went well for them. It was not only orphans and boys from broken homes who went out as young teenagers. Two sixteen-year-old twins, from a happy and well-established middle-class home in Tunbridge Wells, decided to go out on the B.B.M. Scheme in 1957 because National Service was coming to an end and they felt they would otherwise miss their chance of seeing the world. One of the twins said:

I was quite open-minded about whether I would stay. As it turned out, I would like to have stayed. I loved Australia and I had very good job prospects but things worked out differently.

I was the one who really got the idea of going after I saw an advert in the local paper. I got in touch with Australia House and my brother and I put in our applications for the B.B.M. Scheme several months before we were called for an interview. My parents were horrified at first. My older sister had married and gone out to live in Canada and the thought of us going away as well and leaving them on their own was a terrible shock but they agreed to support our application when they realized I was in earnest. I was really the moving force behind it all; my brother always went along with whatever I did then, but he became far more independent when we got to Australia.

At Australia House, where the B.B.M. had their H.Q., my brother and I were interviewed on our own without our parents. We had quite a long interview, at least half an hour, about why we wanted to go to Australia, what kind of work we were hoping to get out there. They never asked us whether we were intending to stay there permanently; I suppose they reckoned we wouldn't know at that stage. We were given a very thorough medical check-up, which we both passed with flying colours, and they also interviewed our parents. They were quite careful about who they took out. They weren't just taking boys with family problems. In fact we were in a group of twelve boys and only two of them seemed to be going for family reasons. Just before we left, we went with our parents to a party at Australia House and on our last night our parents took us all to a West End show. We hadn't been up to London much so it was all very exciting. Mum and Dad wouldn't come down to Southampton, they said they'd be too upset, but they came to see us off at Waterloo and when the train moved out of the station Mum was in floods of tears and even Dad, who was very stiff-upper-lip, was looking distraught. I felt rather guilty that I wasn't more upset but of course we were going off on the biggest adventure of our lives. I didn't realize, until I looked out of the train window, and saw them standing there, looking so broken up, the damage we'd done to them.

I shared a cabin with my brother and about four others and it took us some time to get to know the other B.B.M. boys but, by the end of the voyage, we were all good friends. We were quite sick to begin with, as neither of us had been on a boat before. It took us a couple of weeks to get our sea legs. We were on the *Fairsea* which was a one-class migrant ship. They had packed in as many of us as they could but the food was good. We stopped at Cannes to pick up some French migrants, then we stopped

at Port Said, Suez, Aden and were meant to go to
Fremantle but there was a longshoremen's strike in
Australia, so we were diverted to Singapore because
we needed to stop for fresh water. We stayed there for
a couple of nights and in the end we had to disembark at Melbourne. Our destination was Sydney
but the ship didn't have time to go down there, after
our diversion, so we were flown down from Melbourne in a rather rickety-looking plane, another first for
my brother and me. We were both thrilled and rather
nervous at the prospect of our first flight.

[The brothers went to the B.B.M. hostel in a
suburb of Sydney, and a couple of days later, when
they had settled in, they went to see the B.B.M.
employment officer.] He was an ex-Army officer.
He said that he didn't want to split us up so he had
managed to arrange two jobs for us at a timber
factory. There was an office job and a labouring job.
My brother, Mick, who was much bigger than me
and better built physically, said that I'd better take
the office job and he'd take the labouring job. The
chief accountant who ran the office side of the business was a Big Brother so that's how we probably
got the jobs. The factory was at Mascot, three miles
outside Sydney, right next door to the airport. We
went out there right away for an interview and were
told that we could start work the next week. The
problem was that the hostel was a long way from the
factory so my brother suggested we should go to a
sandwich bar near the factory, and find out if there
was anywhere to stay locally. We went down to this
café and to my surprise Mick, who had never been
the one who set things up in England, got up and
went and asked the lady if there was anywhere we

could stay near by. She said that there might be a possibility of us staying with her and she'd get her brother to give us a ring about it. So we gave her the number at the hostel and her brother rang us up and asked us over for an interview. He came and collected us in his van and we went back to his sister's house where we had a far more strenuous interview than we'd ever had at Australia House. His sister was a divorcee and had one son, who was a bit younger than us, and her brother, who lived near by, was very protective towards her. Anyway we were both approved of, and as the hostel wanted us out by six weeks at the latest – so that there would be room for the new lot of B.B.M. boys when the next ship arrived – we packed our bags and went over there straight away. The hostel provided breakfast and dinner and board free but they liked you to move on when you'd got settled in a job. We went back to the hostel to have a meal with the other boys whom we kept up with. We enjoyed life at the hostel; the food was good, the beds were comfortable and, apart from the fact that we had to have showers outside – and it was in the middle of the Australian winter, which isn't cold like ours, but still quite cool – we found it a pleasant place to live. It was the first time either of us had lived in a house which wasn't our family home. The digs we went into were quite basic; they were just two plainly furnished rooms but we had breakfast and an evening meal and all our clothes washed for us for just four pounds a week. Our weekly wage was then seven pounds a week so that wasn't bad. The divorcee, Mrs G. we called her, and her family – her brothers and sisters and their children who were about our age – became

like a second family to us. They were all mad about
tennis so we used to go and play at her brother's
house – he had a court – and Mrs G.'s son had a car
so we used to go to the beach every weekend.

[They both left the factory when a neighbour of
their landlady's got them jobs at a galvanizing works
at the highly lucrative rate of seven pounds a day.] It
was very hard and dangerous work. You had to
start at five in the morning and we finished at four.
We had to cut our ties with the Big Brother Movement at that time because we would have had to
disclose that we had left the timber factory and taken
on work they would never have approved of. We
had to take the rust off these big iron trollies –
which meant dipping them in an acid bath to get the
rust off and then recoating them in lead and zinc.
The trollies were extremely heavy and the factory
was very hot. The trollies had to be dipped into the
lead and zinc only when they were completely dry.
After we'd been working there about three or four
months one young boy went and put a wet trolley in
and there was this huge explosion. As it was day-to-
day work, none of us had any protection and we were
lucky – neither Mick nor I got hurt – but we decided
to quit the galvanizing works after that.

[In the three months they had been at the works,
the boys had managed to save up five hundred
pounds each which enabled them to go to Brisbane
and have a holiday up there. They also moved out of
Mrs G.'s digs and rented a bungalow with four other
B.B.M. boys.] It was quite a roomy bungalow and
we erected a table-tennis table outside with overhead
lights and played in the evenings. We still went to
the beach every weekend. My brother, Mick, bought

this old car which didn't have a first gear or a reverse but it got us to Brisbane and back and it also got Mick to his girlfriend's house, thirty miles away. He used to go down there once or twice a week. We decided to apply for more conventional jobs. I got a job as a clerk with the Bank of Adelaide at around twelve pounds a week and Mick got a clerical job at one of the big petrol stations – he could type faster than me. We were going our separate ways a lot more by this time, although we still got on very well. I was getting along fine at the bank; we were all having a good time at the bungalow and I was seriously thinking of making my career in Australia – I was doing my first banking exams – when out of the blue I got a call from my sister. She said that Mum was very ill – neither Mum nor Dad had mentioned this in their letter so it came as a complete surprise – and she insisted that Mick and I should return home. Neither of us wanted to go; we'd been in Australia about three years and were both feeling very happy and settled there. Mick was very put out when I told him. 'First you dragged me out here and now you're dragging me back,' he said. He wasn't going to go at first but I managed to persuade him. We had intended just going back for a visit but, having paid our fares back, we got home with hardly any money. I got a transfer to the Bank of Adelaide's branch in London and did the rest of my banking exams in England. Mick joined the Metropolitan Police and, in a few years, we ended up marrying English girls and settling down here. My mother recovered and is still alive, and looking back now I wish I'd never left Australia. I had much better work prospects and it was a better life over there.

Young couples who went out with children usually expected to stay, although some left because of unforeseen circumstances. Sometimes one of the partners, often the wife, could not settle in Australia. In the Fifties wives did not usually work, so they were at home with the children, feeling bored and lonely. Others missed the extended family and found it hard to cope without a grandmother to leave the children with for the odd weekend or a younger sister who could baby-sit if the couple wanted a night out together. Many young wives missed their mothers. Other couples, particularly those with young children, had difficulty getting suitable housing. One couple, who went out with two children aged five and three, found themselves leaving after twelve years in Australia, when they thought they had finally got themselves established. The husband said:

> We went out initially because friends of ours had gone out there and they encouraged us to go. We spent the first months we were there in a hostel in a suburb of Melbourne and I had to walk ten miles to work because there was no public transport near the hostel. Eventually we got out and rented a flat but we couldn't afford any furniture so we used packing cases. My wife had to walk three miles to the kindergarten every day to leave the children there before going off to work. The public transport in Australia is terrible and we couldn't afford to rent a flat and buy a car. After being there a couple of years we were able to rent a private house. In the end we succeeded in obtaining a house from a Housing Commission which meant we didn't have to put down a big deposit; we were able to pay a sort of mortgage

rather than rent, so eventually the house would have been ours. We bought a car and we managed to furnish the house and redecorate it. Then our third child was born and, although my wife was ill for part of the time, we managed quite comfortably for the next three years. Then I became ill and had to have an operation on my vertebrae. I'd got medical insurance so all the medical expenses were covered but afterwards I had to have four months' convalescence. I was a civilian driver for the army so I didn't count as army personnel and they wouldn't pay me any sick leave. Our money ran out and, although we informed the Housing Commission and contacted the Housing Minister and gave them all the facts of our situation, we were told that we would have to move out of our house because our mortgage was in arrears. My wife couldn't work because she was looking after our youngest, who was only three. I had explained to them that I would be back at work in four months' time and I would be able to make up the arrears then but they just weren't interested. We got no compensation for all the decorating and repairs we'd done; we had to sell all our furniture and move to a caravan. In the end we decided to go back to England and relatives at home lent us some money for our return fares. The irony was that, shortly after our return, my wife's uncle died and she got left three thousand pounds which would easily have covered our arrears and left us with a bit of capital. If the inheritance had come through while we were still in Australia, we would never have come back. We're now well-established over here but our daughter, who was about seventeen when we left, returned to Australia to work as a stable hand with race horses and is now married and has a child over there, so our family is split between the two countries.

Sometimes couples would divorce and one half of the family would return to England. Quite frequently children who had been brought up in Australia and had then returned with one or both parents to England would go back to Australia when they were able to support themselves.

Couples often found that the move to Australia brought out new aspects of their personality and this led to them growing apart and going in different directions. It happened to couples of all ages but those who went out when they were still in their teens or twenties were particularly vulnerable. One man went out when he was nineteen and his wife sixteen.

We had a good time on the boat although it was very crowded but when we disembarked at Sydney we were put into a hostel at Dulwich Hill which was right in the middle of the Italian community and we wondered where Australia was. At the hostel, they gave us three weeks to find a job and other accommodation and my wife got a job almost immediately as a secretary. It took me a bit longer but I managed to get a job working on the roads, drilling holes, which I liked because it meant I was out in the sun all day. We rented a flat near the beach and everything was fine for the first eighteen months. Then my wife started to have an affair with her boss, a wealthy American. She'd come from an unhappy home and I think she was looking for someone to look after her. When she told me she was going to leave me it came as a terrible shock. She moved out to live with him and later went with him to America. I was pole-axed. Not having any old friends or family out there, I felt completely lost. I gave up working and just became a beach bum. Then a friend, who owned his own film lighting business, offered me a job and I worked for him for four or five months as a gofer. I met a lot of stunt people and, being fit and athletic, I decided to give it a try and joined a stunt team. I like taking risks and I found, with half a bottle of whisky inside me, I could do anything. You have to have your wits about you if you're being thrown off a horse or over a cliff or out of a helicopter into a shark-infested part of Sydney harbour – I didn't realize till afterwards that it was a particularly bad place for sharks. I found the work totally absorbing and it helped me to forget about my wife. I also started modelling sportswear and evening wear for men in *Vogue* where I met up with an English girl, Lisa, who was one of the sub-editors. She had been asked by a boyfriend to go over to Australia and she had agreed to go if he sent her a ticket. So he did, and she went out there only to discover that he already had a woman living with him. When I first knew her she was in an uncomfortable threesome with both women fighting over this bloke. When I started going out with her, her former boyfriend became very jealous, especially as I kept appearing in all the films he went to see. But Lisa and I got together and are still together. We came back to England when we discovered that she was having a baby, as we thought it would be nice if it was born in Britain. We never got married, although I would like to have done at one stage, because for a long time I di not know whether my first wife had divorced me. I'd lost contact with her since she'd gone to America. I'm now happily settled in Britain but it took me a while to adapt to life here. I missed the outdoor life and the excitement of stunt work – I am now the manager of an estate agency in Surrey. It may seem surprising but I am glad to be back with the drizzle – it never seemed to drizzle in Australia, just poured with rain. I also missed the green grass, the beer and the English people. I missed not being able to go to a friendly English country pub.

Some returned to England because they did not like the Australian climate; in certain areas it can be very hot and dusty and in others, like Melbourne, there are frequent downpours of rain and rapid changes of weather. Others found the Australians coarse and disliked what they considered to be a certain brashness of manner. One man was particularly shocked when he went to work in the outback in Western Australia and found out that once a month the local men went to visit a prostitute who was taken round the towns of the area in the back of a van.

The men I was working with took me along to this run-down suburb where there was a long queue of men waiting behind an old 'ute', a battered utility van. Every five minutes or so one man came out and another went in. By the expressions on their faces, they could all have been waiting to buy ice-cream and it took about as long. When I learnt what the queue was for, I said I hadn't enough money on me (it was only about a couple of pounds) and fled. After that, I began to think there was too big a gulf between me and the Aussies for me to want to live there permanently and I decided to go home.

Some were disillusioned by the reception they received in Australia, particularly at the hostels. Others found their dream of a new life turning into a nightmare. One divorcee in her thirties thought that Australia might provide a better future for her two young children, Joe, aged ten, and Emily, eight.

I went to Australia House and when they heard that I had young children they recommended me to send my children out on a special scheme run by the Church of England. I was sent to see a Miss Jones in an office in Albemarle Street. She told me about this wonderful scheme where my children would be sent out under the auspices of the Church of England Council for Commonwealth and Empire Settlement and would attend a first-rate Australian boarding-school where they would get a free education. Arrangements would be made for me to follow on, not more than six months later, and when I had got myself a job and accommodation the children could come and live with me in the holidays. I was led to believe the boarding-school would be the Australian equivalent of Eton and, as I was hard up after my divorce and concerned about my children's education, I thought it was the best start in life I could give them. I was a bit hesitant about sending the children on ahead on their own but Miss Jones looked at me searchingly and asked me whether I could stand in the way of my children's future and assured me that they would be well looked after. My parents, who were retired army people, also thought the scheme sounded a good one and I showed all the papers to our family solicitor who advised me to go ahead. One of the papers I had to sign was an agreement with the Australian Government that I would not take the children out of Australia until they were twenty-one. As I intended to follow the children out there and for us all to settle in Australia, that did not seem to be a problem.

I saw my son and daughter off – they were then about eight and a half and ten – promising that I would be following in six months' time. They were quite excited at the prospect of seeing Australia and, as they knew that I was coming out to join them there, they weren't too worried. I waited and waited for my ticket to arrive but nothing happened and I never heard anything further from Miss Jones. After writing a number of times, I became concerned and went up to London to see her. I told her that, if I didn't receive my ticket within a month, I would contact my local M.P. and write to the papers about it. My ticket arrived shortly after that.

The children had been sent to what I assumed was a boarding-school near Perth in Western Australia. I had received short notes from the children since they'd arrived but they weren't very communicative. When I eventually arrived in Perth, I found the children weren't in a boarding-school at all but a children's hostel. It was very like an orphanage, in fact there were a few Australian children there from broken homes, but the rest were all British and none of the children's mothers had turned up to claim them. The couple who ran the hostel were very surprised to see me. The clothes I'd sent the children out with – I'd sent them out with a lot of smart clothes which I thought would be suitable for this boarding-school – had all been pooled and the other children were wearing Joe and Emily's clothes. They were all running around in bare feet and the couple who were running the place were using the children as skivvies. They had to wash the floors, clean out the lavatories and do the washing-up. I was horrified; it wasn't at all the kind of future I'd had in mind for Joe and Emily. I discovered that most of the British children had been abandoned by their parents; quite a number were probably the illegitimate offspring of war-time romances and their mothers were glad to get them off their hands. I was told that I was only allowed to take my children out for one weekend a month, from Saturday morning until Sunday evening; the other weekends I had to visit them in the home.

I managed to get a job as a clerk with the local police department which provided enough money for me to be able to support the children. Another lady at work had a bungalow and wanted someone to share it with her. It had three bedrooms and she agreed that I could have one and the children could have the other. I went to the home and told them that I had a job and accommodation for the children and that I wanted them to come and live with me. They asked me what time I got back from work and I told them that I finished work at five-thirty and would be back at the bungalow by six o'clock at the latest. They told me I couldn't have the children to live with me because there would be no one to look after them when they got back from school – around four o'clock – until six. They would not listen when I pointed out that my children were quite sensible and that I would give them a latchkey and they would be able to ring me at work if there were any problems. But the couple at the hostel refused point blank. It was then that I decided to take the children back to England. I knew that they wanted to live with me and I couldn't face the prospect of them staying on in that home. Then I realized I'd signed this agreement with the Australian Government that the children would stay in Australia until they were twenty-one. I went to the Government offices in Perth and pointed out that I had signed the agreement on false pretences. I'd been told that the conditions my children would be living in would be quite different from what I actually found when I turned up there. After a great deal of wrangling, I finally got the children's passports and we all went back to live with my parents. The moment I got back to England, I tried to put the whole thing behind me; it just seemed like a bad dream.

Her son, Joe, had mixed feelings about his two years in Australia. He had disliked the couple who ran the home but he enjoyed the beaches and the weather, and found it quite easy to settle in and make friends with the other children. Unlike his mother, he also found it less difficult to adapt to a reality that was different from the one he had expected.

I was looking forward to the trip when I first heard about it. I had been told that I was going to a boarding-school very much along the English public school lines and, as we were literally struggling then, it seemed like a good idea. My father separated from my mother when I was three and had gone to Africa to join the Kenyan police. He did not communicate with my mother and we had no financial support from him so it had been difficult. My grandparents were always very supportive but they were living on a pension so they couldn't do much to help us with our education, although they had us to live with them and were very kind. My mother was concerned because the state schools near my grandparents' house were not at all good. The whole education system was recovering from the effect of the War and I think my mother thought we'd have a better chance of a good career if we were educated in Australia. I didn't feel very bothered about leaving my mother because I knew she was going to follow us out and both my sister and I enjoyed the voyage. For a boy, it was exciting being on board ship and, even as children, we were both quite independent. When we got to the home, which was a rather ramshackle house very close to the beach, just outside Fremantle, we were both surprised. It wasn't quite the posh boarding-school that we'd had in mind but we were allowed down to the beach every weekend and could go swimming and I loved all of that. The only really bad thing about the home was the people who ran it. The husband was always making us do jobs for him and he treated us like servants – we did all the washing and cleaning and the dirty jobs at the home. His wife did the cooking and she was a dreadful cook so the food was pretty awful but there was always plenty of it. Most of the children were quite afraid of this couple; there was always a sense of tension when they were around but we had some good times together when we were on our own. There was also this special society of people who were friends of the home and they would lay on

these wonderful barbecues for us about once every
three months. We were all given huge steaks which
was a great treat for us as the rest of the time we had
nothing but second-rate cuts of lamb. For Christmas
we were boarded out with local people, who were
part of this society, and I was sent to a very nice
family with boys around my age and thoroughly
enjoyed it. During term-time we went by bus to the
local state school, which didn't have a very good
education; in fact when we got back to England, my
sister and I found that we'd fallen behind the rest of
our age group. Like most of Australian life, the
school in Perth was very easy-going; all our energies
went on our outdoor life.

When my mother arrived, things were different.
We'd become more independent by then because
we'd been nearly a year on our own but of course
we wanted to go and live with her and have a home
life again. Although we always thought she'd come
because she wrote to us regularly and told us she
was coming over, we realized that lots of children in
the home had been waiting for their mothers for
ages and they'd never turned up. Once the couple
got us all together and told us we didn't have families
anymore, we belonged to the State of Western Australia, but I didn't really believe them.

A lot of the children in the home had come from
very poor families and, although some of them
would get homesick and miss their parents, quite a
few had never known what it was like not to feel
hungry and to be in a climate where they seldom felt
cold. The summers were beautiful and the winters
were always quite mild; we all became very healthy
with the outdoor life and the sea air. When my

mother decided to go back to England I was glad but both my sister and I had got to like Australia. Later, when she was grown up, my sister quite seriously considered emigrating to Australia and making a life there but she got married to an American and went to live in the States.

Looking back now I'm glad I went out there. It made me better at coping on my own. It also gave me a taste for travel. When I left school, I joined the Royal Marines and went out to Borneo. I think the trip to Australia gave me a longing for adventure. I'd learnt to cope with the unexpected and I enjoyed the challenge.

Many of those who did not settle still felt that Australia had broadened their horizons. Their time out there had enabled them to do things, meet people and have experiences that they would never have had if they had stayed at home.

CONCLUSION

By the end of the 1950s there were a number of different schemes available to British migrants. The Bring-out-a-Briton Scheme was introduced in 1957 and the Nest Egg Scheme started soon after. The aim of the Bring-out-a-Briton Scheme was to encourage businesses and service organizations to sponsor British migrants. Under this scheme the Rotary and the Apex clubs sent out people whom they sponsored and so did a number of business associations. A migration officer, who helped to organize the Scheme when it first started, said, 'We provided all the assisted passages but we wanted other organizations to encourage people to come here by arranging accommodation for them in Australia, finding them jobs and generally rallying round to help them settle.'

The push to attract more Britons came after the slump in emigration in the mid-Fifties when Australia went through a minor depression. The biggest influx of British migrants to Australia came at the beginning and end of the decade. Nearly 34,000 British migrants went out in 1959, the highest total since 1952. By the late Fifties Britain was more prosperous and there were more job opportunities available in the UK so special schemes, like the Bring-out-a-Briton, were set up to attract those who might have been put off by stories of the hostels and other difficulties of settling in Australia. More migration offices were opened in industrial towns

'Actually we planned to go to Brighton, but we didn't have the money'

in the U K and Northern Ireland, and the conditions for providing assisted passages to British immigrants were made easier than they had ever been before. Many British-assisted migrants were given passage by air at the same nominal fee (ten pounds) as applied to sea passage. Those who went out under these sponsored schemes knew they would be provided with decent accommodation and a good job and that they would not have to struggle to achieve the standard of living they had left behind in Britain. Many of those who went out under these schemes were business or professional people whose working prospects in Britain were already good and who needed to be persuaded that there would be a still better life for them in Australia.

'By the end of the Fifties we were looking for a different type of migrant,' said another migration officer.

Make it easier . . . help build Australia

BRING OUT A BRITON

To make Australia greater, richer, stronger, we must develop the country by expanding industry and primary production. By widening employment opportunities we raise the standards of living for all.

Part of the answer to a greater Australia is a greater population. We *must* have more people . . . more migrants who are

● *Skilled, for trades, industry and technical advancement.*

● *Semi-skilled, for occupations demanding workers.*

● *Unskilled, for labour on rugged projects.*

The Commonwealth Government has a major assisted-passages scheme to "Bring out a Briton" which requires the migrant to pay only £10 Sterling for his total fare. The

scheme provides two main categories under which the Australian public can *actively* help to bring out more British migrants.

PERSONAL NOMINATION. Australians may nominate friends and relatives in Britain for assisted passages. The sponsor pays nothing, but he must provide initial living accommodation.

GROUP NOMINATION. Australian employers, including State instrumentalities, may nominate the type of workers they need. Most of these migrants are single men and women. The intending employer must provide living accommodation. The Commonwealth also operates its own scheme to bring out more British migrants.

Make further detailed enquiries to-day!

'We no longer wanted just any healthy young people who would stay and have families in Australia, we wanted people with specific skills who would make a valuable contribution to the work force.'

The Nest Egg Scheme allowed families with five

hundred pounds or more to qualify for the Assisted Passage Scheme without having a sponsor, on condition that they would make their own arrangements for accommodation on arrival in Australia. It was for the migrants on these kinds of schemes that Australian housing companies began to set up offices in Britain. Along with the banks, which offered special services to migrants who wanted business loans or needed to have their capital transferred to Australia, the housing companies also had special officers to advise migrants. Often representatives from banks and from the housing companies would accompany a migration information officer when he went to give a talk to a group interested in the Ten Pound Fare.

One ex-housing-company information officer said:

We were kind of unofficially part of the Scheme. Representatives from the big housing companies would attend information meetings for the general public that were set up by the Australian Immigration Department. Their information officers, representatives from some of the banks, and some of us would all go to these which were held in town halls or anywhere we could have a large gathering. These meetings were usually very popular and attracted big audiences. First there would be a film show about Australia; then the audience would be able to come to the different booths that we had set up and get all the necessary information on everything related to migration. The information officers from the housing companies would provide details about the cost of living in different parts of Australia, types of houses available and they would be able to arrange for a family to buy a house in Australia before they left England. There were also freight companies which organized the transfer of all the family's furniture and effects. It was cheaper to ship everything over there than to start all over again and get replacements in Australia.

There were special schemes set up to encourage graduates to migrate and there were schemes sponsored by the different churches. The migrants who went out on these schemes often had a much easier time settling in than those who went to the hostels. They usually found they could resume a normal life, having been settled into a home and a job, far quicker than the migrants who had to establish themselves independently.

Although the drive for the better educated migrant became more pronounced in the late Fifties, Australia had decided, early on in its development of an immigration policy, that immigrants should be selected to provide a skilled and balanced workforce. Some British people were concerned at the idea of the young and the skilled leaving Britain and feared that it would become over-populated with the middle-aged and O A Ps. One anxious reader wrote to the *Spectator* as early as 12 September 1947:

Whilst we all are deeply indebted and grateful to Australia, Canada, New Zealand, South Africa etc. for their really magnificent help in our present – and in our past – difficulties, we must not let ourselves be blinded to the serious position the present form of emigration is causing. We must never forget that we are an over-populated country with an increasing percentage of old people. We lost many of our young people in the late war, many more are daily emigrating and many thousands more wish to go as soon as transport is available. It is a tragic mistake to try to remove the bogies of over-population here and under-population in the Dominions by simply allowing the emigration of these many thousands of young people. The idea of middle-aged and aged people starting life anew in a strange land may seem far from attractive, but this is the only solution to our problem; emigration of whole families (i.e., several generations) must take place and this be logically extended to the emigration of whole towns and villages.

Although nothing quite as extreme as this took place, a considerable number of elderly relations of young couples who emigrated either accompanied their children or followed them out later; often one family would be encouraged to emigrate because their next-door neighbours, relations or friends had gone out before them and had written back to tell them that life was indeed better down-under.

An editorial note in the *Spectator* of 30 July 1948 echoes the same fears:

There is . . . one question of vital concern both to us and to Australians about which there has been much thought, some talk, but little information, and this is emigration. Mr Chiffley said at a press conference in London that 'the fullest understanding exists between the British and the Australian Governments on this matter', and the Government's attitude was later defined by Mr Gordon-Walker as being 'to encourage and facilitate the flow of emigration from this island to the various parts of the Commonwealth', provided only that we do not lose too many skilled workers in certain categories. But this benevolent attitude can only act as a substitute for a policy as long as the shortage of shipping makes any more ambitious plan impossible. The Australian Minister for Immigration, less hesitant, looks ahead to the settling of 20 million newcomers within the next two generations, most of whom are expected to be provided by the British Isles. Presumably we, on our side, agree that our island is overpopulated or we would not allow the present exodus of about 75,000 emigrants a year. But sooner or later we have got to make up our minds to what extent we are overpopulated and to what extent our capacity to keep our heads above water is going to be improved by allowing many of our most enterprising young men and women to leave us for good. What sort of an island population do we look for at the end of the century? A few aged remittance-men? Or something a bit more vigorous? We must decide without any delay not only whom we can spare, but on what grounds we can spare them.

By 1951, when it became evident that Britain would not be the only source of migrants and that many Europeans and displaced persons were helping to swell Australia's immigration numbers, the *Spectator* takes a more relaxed tone towards British emigration although, at that time, it still looked as though the majority of New Australians would be British:

A speech made by the Australian Minister for Immigration this week (January 26, 1951) indicates

'Come and make yourself at home. I rather like you'

the practical and considered policy Australia is pursuing in the matter of attracting new citizens. She needs a larger population, and a balanced population. The immediate requirement is for skilled workers rather than unskilled labourers, and it is proposed to draw them from the United Kingdom, Germany, Holland and Italy, as well as from Displaced Persons centres; the total contemplated for 1951 being 200,000. These are wise and enlightened plans – as it was wise and enlightened to appoint a special Minister for Immigration in the first instance. Australia is determined to remain essentially British, and nothing in her immigration policy threatens that. Out of a population of 8,200,000 last June all but the odd 200,000 ranked as British and at the present rate of immigration nine persons out of ten will be British in 1960. Australia has the experience of the greatest of all 'reception' countries, the United States, to learn from. Even there, though immigration was heterogeneous and unrestricted till the beginning of this century, assimilation has on the whole been adequate. In Australia's case there will be both limitation and selection, and the newcomers should be integrated into the national society without difficulty or delay. The decision to attract 25,000 Germans a year is particularly sound, for Germans make extremely good settlers.

In spite of careful planning, Australia's immigration policy did not go quite as smoothly as predicted in this editorial and the immigration numbers fluctuated quite considerably, depending on the state of the Australian economy. The forecast that by 1960 nine out of ten of Australia's immigrants would be British was still further off the mark, although in the early 1950s it might well have looked as though that prediction would come true. In fact, by the 1960s, economic conditions in Britain had improved considerably and interest in emigration had begun to fall off. The Australians were turning more and more to other European countries to fill their immigration quotas.

The Australian Government's decision to let all children under nineteen years of age who were members of a nominated family have free passages shows how keen the Australians were to continue with the Assisted Passage Scheme in Britain, although it was now only a small part of their overall policy.

There was a rush to migrate during the post-war depression in Britain, but what was it in the more

prosperous late Fifties that still attracted British migrants to Australia? Some of those interviewed, who
went out in the late Fifties, often went for a number of
different reasons, some personal and some more general. The Australian climate and the availability of jobs
always remained predominant reasons for families to
think of emigrating. By the end of the decade there
were also more people joining friends or relations who
had gone out earlier. More young single people realized
that it was the perfect way to see the world and have a
two-year working-holiday, especially those who realized
that they would not be called up for National Service.
Couples, concerned about their children's future, often
decided to emigrate, although they might not have
done so in other circumstances. Quite a number of
young couples made the decision to emigrate reluctantly but felt convinced that their children had the
chance of a better future in a freer, more classless
society. They thought that Britain, with its exclusive
public school network and class distinctions, limited
particular types of jobs to the select few.

One aspect of Australia which migrants of all ages
and classes often liked was the sense of freedom and
the feeling of space. Those who had felt restricted in
Britain by their social class, or their family relationships, or the prying eyes of neighbours, or just a
general expectation of conformity to a particular set of
social mores, often felt a wonderful sense of release in
Australia. One nineteen-year-old boy, who emigrated
with his parents, left a council house on an estate in
Newcastle for a flat in Perth. He made friends with a
gang of Australian teenagers and discovered the plea-
sures of barbecues out in the bush and parties on the
beach, an outdoor life he had never known in Britain:

Just about every weekend we'd borrow one of the blokes' father's cars and stick a five-gallon keg of beer in the back and go down to the beach and have a beach party. There were about twenty of us. We'd have a big fire down on the beach and there was this little shop down there – it was the only shop around there, the rest was bush – and the chap who lived on the premises of the shop, he used to know when we were coming up and he would have steak and sausages, which we bought off him and made ourselves a barbecue. We'd hire radios so there was plenty of music and everyone did just what they wanted. If you wanted to have a swim, you had a swim, if you wanted to drink beer, you drank beer, if you wanted to do something else, you did something else . . . They were good days, those days. I can't really compare it with what it was like back in England – the climatic conditions are so different for a start and money seemed to go further over here. I couldn't have bought a car back in England, for instance, which I did by the time I was twenty-one. You were quite fortunate to have a motorbike in England. To be quite frank with you, financially, since I've come out to Australia, I haven't looked back. I've got a much better life-style over here and it's also freer, easier – over in England you're too closely knit together. If you stopped to talk to somebody down the street, the whole street would know about it. Tongues would start wagging, 'Is he having it off with her?' Here I don't know what my neighbours are doing and I don't want to know.

Day-to-day life is quite different here. Housewives, for instance, are much more likely to go off early to the supermarket and get everything they need and then go down to the beach or spend the day in the country, whereas in England everyone lived on each other's doorsteps and they'd spend half the blooming day nattering to their next-door neighbour.

Another migrant summed up much the same feelings in words which many of those who have settled and made their homes in Australia, would agree with: 'I love the freedom of Australia. It's so relaxed here, there's no pomp and ceremony.'

Many regarded their Ten Pound Fare as the best investment of their lives. It offered them a way out of a failed marriage or a dead-end job; a chance to meet new people and explore new continents; the possibility of unlimited success – and sometimes unforeseen failure – and a means of discovering more about themselves. As one Ten Pound Pom said: 'Whatever happened, whether you went and settled or whether you only went for the two years, the experience changed you. You weren't the same person who first boarded the ship at Southampton for a mysterious destination on the other side of the world.'

INDEX

INDEX

INDEX

INDEX